# The Fabulous PANDA

## Michael de Havilland

*The Giant Panda is one of the world's most unique, fascinating and certainly lovable of all creatures. With the march of time its destiny has become beset with a number of rare problems that do not affect other members of the Animal Kingdom. It is to be hoped that readers beyond the mountains and shores of Mother China will make interesting and useful discoveries in this book.*

Prof. Hu Jin Chu
Field Director
Save the Panda Operation
Sichuan

# The Fabulous PANDA
## Michael de Havilland

*illustrated with photographs*

A Pan Original
Pan Books  London and Sydney

*To Laura, Ashley, Lance and 'Dimbleby'*

First published 1987 by Pan Books Ltd
Cavaye Place, London SW10 9PG

9 8 7 6 5 4 3 2 1

© Michael de Havilland 1987

ISBN 0 330 29661 2

Photoset by Parker Typesetting Service, Leicester
Printed and bound in Great Britain by
Springbourne Press Ltd, Basildon, Essex.

Designed and edited by Treld Bicknell


Maps by Creative Cartography

Drawings by Lorna Turpin

Calligraphy byMr Yang Bingchuan

The photographs have come from many sources, many of them in
China. The author and publishers wish to thank the following for
providing illustrative material:
Zhang Shuicheng; Li Di; Gou Gogiang; Pu Tao; Song Guangmeng;
*China Reconstructs*; *China Daily*; *China Pictorial*, Foreign Language
Press; Science Press; Beijing Zoo, Veno Zoo, Japan; Madrid Zoo (L.
Dominquez); Professor Chu Ching; Mr Bob Edmonds; Mr J. Michael
McGean; Peking Slide Studios and the World Wildlife Fund. Thanks
are also due to the Library of the Museum of Natural History, Paris
for page 25; Brookfield Zoo, Chicago for page 32; The Smithsonian
Institution, Washington DC for pages 33 and 41; Bruce Coleman Ltd.
for pages 26 *above* (photographer Stephen Krasemann) and *below*
(photographer Bob and Clara Calhoun) and 106 (photographer Gerald
Cubitt); National Zoological Park, Washington DC (photographer
Jessie Coheb) for page 93; Parc Zoologique, Paris for page 97 *above*;
BBC Hulton Picture Library for page 98 and the Zoological Board of
Control, St Louis for page 99.

# Contents

*Animals are not brethren, they are not underlings; they are other nations, caught with ourselves in the net of life and time ...*

Henry Beeston

*All young people should learn about the mysterious pandas ... the only major mammals of China to survive the Ice Age, the only ones which changed from an all-carnivorous to an herbivorous diet, and, of course, the only ones with that unique colouring which endears them to all hearts ...*

Prof. Wang Hsien-peng
Academica Sinica
Beijing

# Introduction

Pandas had never at any time been remotely in my mind, even though I once founded the Guernsey Zoo in the mid-1960s. With hindsight it seems that destiny singled me out to make that memorable 2,500-kilometre train journey from Shanghai to Chongqing to celebrate the new Monkey Year of February 1980; a visit that would result in this book.

Chongqing, formerly blitzed by the Japanese, was still in turmoil of belated reconstruction. Cement bricks and unfinished buildings cluttered the scene – and it was freezing cold. To kill the initial boredom, I spent the first three days at the Chongqing Zoo. Its panda attendant tried his best to convince me that, if his charges lived in the wild, they would perish without a daily diet of some five hundred stems of bamboo.

'You're surely not serious. That's a colossal amount.'

His thin smile was almost patronising as if he thought, 'these foreigners don't know a damn thing.'

A welcome sun came out and warmed the city. I began to explore. Perched terrifyingly near the edge of towering limestone cliffs, I found it to be criss-crossed by a network of hair-raising ladder streets that plunged dramatically toward the confluence of the Great River, alias Son of the Ocean (the Yangtze), and the Jialing River, a rendezvous aptly named Double Jubilation. In the sharp sunlight their waters intermingled like molten gold before breaking free in a frenetic rush to the East China Sea, 4,200 kilometres away. The scene bustled with junks and sampans.

I panted up steep hills smothered in huddles of derelict shacks, with packs of gaping children, no doubt awed at the oddity of a 'longnose' in their midst, following at my heels. Then, at the summit, I found myself in front of a Gothic-style church which towered above the shambles of low, crouching houses.

Oddly, two Union Jack designs were beautifully carved into the granite facade. A British church? At that moment leaving the church was a little old lady, wizened and lined and, I quickly noted, with bound feet. To my further astonishment she said in perfect French, 'Are you looking for someone, monsieur?'

As French is my mother tongue this presented no problem. I asked if the church was British.

She flashed an understanding smile. 'This is the Church of St Joseph. It was founded in the 1890s by the *Missions d'Etrangères de Paris*,' she explained. 'No one knows how the British flag design ever came to be there because this church has always been French, which is the reason why most of the congregation speak French.'

I could have said a courteous *au revoir* and left, but something made me ask to look at the handsome Missal she was carrying. The fly leaf bore a faded signature in Chinese characters.

'That is Père David's signature.' Her voice was soft.

My expression bought a smile to her dark eyes. 'There was only one Père David, a holy saint if ever there was one,' she said in a hushed tone.

By late afternoon sitting in her unheated stone-floored home, the cold so piercing that my stockinged feet were wrapped in the sheepskin lining of my coat, I had listened to her story in fascinated silence. Her great-grandfather, a hunter, had been the famous missionary's first Chinese convert, in Christmas week 1864. Thereafter he acompanied him on his last two China expeditions from 1866 to 1874. But her own father, too, had also been a hunter, the chief assistant to the legendary Mr Smith.

Mr Smith? Who was he – and why legendary?

More fascinating facts spilled out. Mr Smith had made five expeditions, and had had many 'panda triumphs'. But when she began to describe his feat of taking six pandas through war-torn China in the summer of 1938, I could not resist murmering, 'How could he have done so? Your Chongqing Zoo tell me that a panda needs at least five hundred pieces of bamboo a day for its survival, so how—?

She interrupted softly. 'Did you not know that he arrived in England with five of them alive after a journey of ninety-five days?'

I felt like screaming BUT HOW?

And then I was going through the pages of a diary this 'Mr Smith' had left behind which told the secret, and admiring a silver cigarette case he had given her father when he left China for the last time. For some time her parting words began to haunt me. 'Mr Smith's adventures would make an interesting book.'

Nearly three years later at Tokyo's colourful Ueno Zoo Park, my memory was whipped back by the voice of an American teacher with some students grouped round the panda enclosure watching 'Huan-Huan' and 'Fei-Fei' romping and squealing. 'Someone should write a book about pandas from A to Z,' he lamented. 'Pretty-pretty picture books tell us far too little!'

At that second in time something clicked in my mind. I could hear Lo Feng-di's words . . . 'an interesting book'.

Well, why not? And so began an interest which soon became a passion . . .

M de H, 1987

---

*Note*: Within these pages the name Beijing appears frequently. What is or where is it? Beijing is simply the Chinese name for their capital Peking . . . as we call ours London; the Americans call theirs Washington; the French, Paris and so on. In Chinese the letter P is always pronounced B, and a K becomes J. Elsewhere modern spellings for Chinese names have been used throughout.

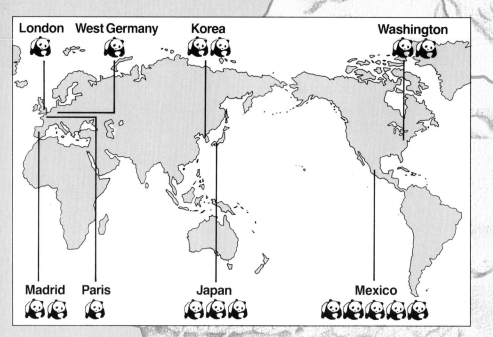

London    West Germany     Korea       Washington

Madrid    Paris       Japan       Mexico

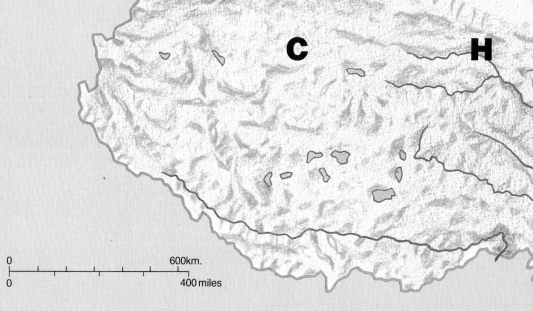

C       H

0       600km.

0       400 miles

 Early distribution of Panda populations

 Today's concentration of Panda populations

BURMA

MONGOLIA

*The once-upon-a-time distribution of the Giant Panda in the wild compared with today's rapidly diminishing population, based on a map by Grace Richmond and, inset, zoo Pandas outside China.*

Beijing

Xi'an

Shanghai

Chang Jiang
(Yangtze)

Chengdu

SICHUAN
Chongqing

HONG KONG

## Acknowledgements

MY THANKS ARE DUE TO THE FOLLOWING: PROFESSOR HU JIN CHU, tireless field director of operations at Wolong Reserve where the Chinese and the World Wildlife Fund are collaborating in massive research to help save the endangered species; Mr Zhang Shuicheng who was largely responsible for many of the exciting panda photographs, his small son Xiao Nan and his assistant Miss O. Yanggan; Professor Chu Ching, Director of the Institute of Zoology Academia Sinica, for data and illustrations of the panda's spectacular jaw and dental structure; my former interpreter Mr Bao Hsien-ping of Shangai, and Mr Wang Kaitu, a past student of mine, of Chongqing; Mr Li Yangwen, Director of Beijing Zoo, and the directors of the Chengdu and Shangai Zoos. Staff reporters from *China Reconstructs*, *China Pictorial*, *China Daily* and the *Beijing Review* proved to be goldmines of information on the latest events in Pandaland. And the United States Consul-General at Chengdu, Mr William W. Thomas, Jr, took great pains to do some checking on my behalf.

From beyond the shores of Cathay, the WWF provided a plethora of helpful facts; while Mr D. McClintock, the International Dendrology Society's editor; Mrs Jane Stubbs and Mrs Anne Henry at the Royal Botanical Gardens, Kew, and the American Bamboo Society between them gave invaluable assistance on matters relating to the mysterious bamboo. For the events of Père David's Second China Expedition, 1868–1872, which uncovered for the Western world the existence of panda life, my thanks go to Père G. Baldaccino and Père Jean Verinaud, Archivists of the Lazarist Order and *Les Missions Etrangères de Paris* respectively; the Paris Natural History Museum; the Mayor of Espelette where the David family lived; and also to Madame Yvonne Combes, Famille Nowak and Famille Miniscloux, of Montrouge (Paris), Barentin and Chartres respectively. I am also indebted to the BBC Archives, BBC Publications; Mr Andrew Currant, of the British Museum's Dept of Palaeontology (Fossil Mammal Section); the Glen and Blue Funnel Lines; Miss Deborah Lindsay at Maritime House (Records) Liverpool; Miss K. Langrish, Lloyds Register of Shipping; Mr Melvyn Barnes, Director of the City of London Libraries and Art Galleries; the Hong Kong Public Records Office; Mr A. MacDermott of the British Embassy at Tokyo; Mr Steven P. Johnson, Archivist Librarian of the New York Zoological Society; Mr Paul

12

Grey, Assistant Director for Military Records at St Louis, and to the Registrar of Brompton Hospital.

I am more than grateful to Professor Heinz-Georg Klos, Director of West Berlin Zoo, for drawing my attention to the informative Proceedings of the First International Symposium on the Giant Panda held at Berlin, 1984. More facts came from the panda zoos of London, Paris, Madrid and Washington DC, and the zoos of Los Angeles and San Francisco, who had been loaned a pair of pandas by the Chinese Government in 1984. Thanks to Mr J. Michael McGean, at Dartmouth College, New Hampshire, for taking pains to make a copy of the earliest known photograph of Tangier Smith, taken in 1904, and to the Field Museum and Brookfield Zoo, both of Chicago, and the St Louis Zoo for their fascinating stories where they were making panda history long, long, before pandas were being displayed anywhere in the world – including China!

That was about the time of this 'Mr Smith's' private saga, which would climax at snow-bound Tilbury within hours of Christmas Eve 1938, when dockers were flabbergasted to see FIVE giant pandas being off-loaded from a ship just in from China.

Before the book was finally finished, there were still wide gaps in his story. My dilemma was how to contact any surviving members of the Tangier Smith clan. As he had once been a banker I tried endless bank archives but in vain. No one seemed to know anything about this seemingly ghost figure from the past. Eventually, an ad in the Personal Column of the *Daily Telegraph* ... 'Vital information wanted about Floyd Tangier Smith, legendary king of panda hunters in China ...' did the trick. The 'phone rang that evening. Mr and Mrs Gerald Hodgson of Claygate, Surrey, advised me to write to a kinswoman of theirs, Dr Ruth Tangier Smith, MD of Portola Valley, California. Within two months this section of the panda jigsaw was complete.

One curious coincidence is almost too hard to believe. Having chased round in China and parts of France on the Père David leg of the story, I was to find that the famous missionary's great-grand nephew, Mr Bob Edmonds, lived only a matter of thirty kilometres from my home in Sussex!

Last, but by no means least, Mr Paul Mosely and his wife Xiaomo, of Beijing.

# PART I
# IN THE PAST

# CHAPTER ONE

# The Beginning

*Pandas thrive in snow conditions*

THE ORIGINS OF THE GIANT PANDA HAVE THEIR ROOTS in the far distant past. It evolved to inhabit fruitfully a quarter of the huge Chinese Empire where it became the only major species of mammal to survive the Ice Age in China. Having survived the vicissitudes of this glacial period, it seems like a deliberate twist of irony – with overtones of a dark conspiracy – that a number of other factors have since spiralled into a massive threat to its existence. Its numbers have been decimated and its habitat shrunk to a tiny corner of this vast country.

Sophisticated science and technology – which can put men on the moon, probe willy-nilly into the secrets of outer space and beget artificially-inseminated humans – seem almost mockingly impotent to stave off the ungovernable forces that imperil the panda's survival and threaten it with extinction.

Today, however, a small ray of hope at long last illuminates the future. The Chinese, traditionally known for their Confucian, unhurried life-style, have bestirred themselves with uncharacteristic vigour. Nothing is being left undone, no 'stone unturned' and no expense spared to save the world's darling from sharing the fate of the dodo. The green sprawl of the bamboo forests and mountains which all pandas inhabit is now a hive of scientific activity.

The purpose of this book is to inform, as well as entertain, the Western reader (who is normally familiar with little more than depressing headlines of the animal's plight or winsome pictures of posing pandas) of the enormous and complex dangers by which the Giant Panda is ruthlessly trapped and threatened. Its aim is also to help the reader understand and appreciate the degree of co-operation between dedicated and compassionate Chinese and foreign scientists seconded by a supportive World Wildlife Fund who are researching the panda's life and environment in order to help it through its evolutionary crisis and so survive as a species.

From where and when did this remarkable creature, a unique and irreplaceable legacy, originate?

The Giant Panda is called a 'living fossil', being the last surviving member of a line of descent that branched off so long ago that *it is now untraceable*. However, fossil records *do* show that the panda developed into a recognizable species about two million years ago during the Pleistocene Age, but otherwise little is known about the mystery of its origins. For even the earliest fossils share its present-day characteristics – a thick skeleton with unusually massive jaws and cheekbones, and an impressive set of teeth which include the largest molars of any animal (proving its carnivorous heritage now long since adapted to an exclusive diet of bamboo and other fibrous plants). It is, however, a fallacy that the recurring bamboo famines constitute the panda's sole enemy. If only it were that simple!

Fossil bones discovered in the last hundred years show that pandas existed 700,000 years ago in great profusion to within less than a hundred and fifty kilometres of Beijing, down into the deep south to within sight of Hong Kong and then in a westward sweep across to the Tibetan highlands.

It is perhaps not so surpising, then, that panda skulls have been found buried as funerary relics in many ancient tombs of China. One, it has been claimed, was buried with the First Emperor, Ch'in Shih-Huang-Di, who in 213 BC had accepted the tribute gift of a pelt and carcass from a visiting Duke of Sichuan. Classical chroniclers for centuries described the mysterious pandas in their writings.

The Chinese, then, had every reason to believe that this unique animal was wholly indigenous to

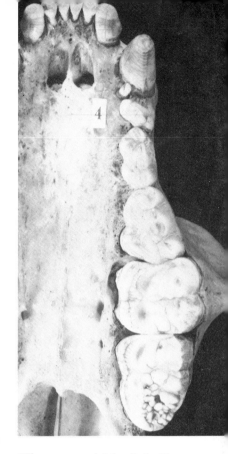

*The great width of skull across the cheekbones is responsible for the massive molars and jaw muscles which make it possible for the panda to 'steamroller' through the toughest of bamboo cane, which not even the most powerful human hands can snap at a single try. The molars are remarkable not only for their great size, but also for the large number of bead-like cusps, almost like cog wheels, round the base of this tooth and the molar in front. These are not to be found in any other mammal.*

17

*The high and wide open spaces which have been the pandas' habitat since the beginning of time.*

*He may appear to be lost in his vast surroundings, but pandas never migrate but keep to their home territory of about six or seven square kilometres.*

China. Was it any wonder then, that they were astonished to learn in 1913, that a British biologist, A. L. Bacon, digging in a cavern at the Burmese ruby mine town of Mogok, had discovered the fossils of Giant Pandas? They were perfect specimens! Since 1914, *Aelureidopus baconi*, a skull with a detached tooth, has been on display at the British Museum.

Despite the mysterious existence of the silent, solitary pandas their presence was no secret to the Chinese of any area of that far-flung country, not even to those who lived far, far beyond the green oceans of the animals' bamboo habitat.

The *Shi Jing*, China's earliest *Book of Historical Records*,* which chronicles the nation's history and major events as far back as 4,000 years and is reputed for its meticulous accuracy, cited the panda as a strange semi-divine animal so rarely seen by the human eye that it became known as the 'hermit of the forests'.

In AD 760 that unrivalled giant of a Tang poet, Du Fu, a resident of Chengdu, the walled capital of Sichuan, in the heart of panda land, expressed the opinion that the panda was so empowered by Heaven to exorcise evil spirits that one had only to paint its face on to a wooden screen and prop it up against one's front door to enjoy immunity from the devil's disciples. Such screens became a common sight.

But down through the centuries no whisper of the Giant Panda's presence ever penetrated to the world

---

*The author was Sa Mi Qian, historiographer for Emperor Wu in the second century BC. He based his work on the Imperial archives from the beginning of China to his day. Every word was written in prison, he having incurred royal displeasure. Sa's grave at his birthplace Zhi Chuan is the most important in China after that of Confucius and called Tai Shi Qi, or Funerary Temple of the Great Chronicler.

beyond that secretive Middle Kingdom.

It did not even reach the ears of Marco Polo, that much-favoured son of the Imperial court and endowed by Kublai Khan with seventeen years of privileged access to any part of China he fancied. Nor those of the Jesuit cartographers who also spent seventeen painstaking years covering the hundreds of counties to prepare and publish their historic first map of China. As for the all-knowledgeable Theophine Pinchon, French Bishop of Chengdu, whose diocese sprawled the length and breadth of 'Panda Province' itself, and was staffed with a team of sharp-eyed missionaries who never failed to report to him the slightest happening in their 'parishes', he could not have known – or Rome would assuredly have been informed. The mystery is how they failed to notice the panda door gods, though perhaps the logical explanation is that they were only put out when darkness fell.

Suddenly, in the mid-nineteenth century, the fateful curve of destiny directed the footsteps of a modest country cleric from France to a discovery that was to astonish and enchant an incredulous world.

*The pandas' vast habitat of mountains, valleys, rivers.*

# CHAPTER TWO

# Père David

*The globe-trotting biologist in retirement at Espelette, his Basque home town.*

FROM OBSCURITY A PRIEST KNOWN AS PÈRE DAVID SHOT to the pinnacle of the international field of wildlife study by successfully completing a series of astonishing expeditions never attempted before; and not merely in Asia, but also in South America, North Africa, Europe and Asia Minor. His Chinese gifts to the Paris Natural History Museum alone totalled nearly 16,000 different species, at least one-fifth of them new to Western eyes. They included 3,425 botanical species, 10,165 entomological species, 633 mammals and 1,361 birds as well as the eggs of fifty-nine rare species.

His achievements were publicly noted by Pope Leo XIII, earned him the Gold Medal of the French Geographic Society, a seat in the Academy of Sciences and a professorship, along with a string of other honours. At the age of seventy-two, when he was still globe trotting in the cause of natural science, France conferred on him its highest accolade, Grand Officer of the Legion of Honour. Even the Chinese Emperor – gratefully acknowledging the gift of a museum at Beijing stocked with the rarest of specimens – paid him the compliment of referring to this 'most remarkable barbarian'.

Jean-Pierre Armand, born 7 September 1826, in the village of Espelette near Bayonne, was fortunate in having a doctor father, Dominique David, who encouraged his son to pursue an interest in nature study. As a schoolboy he had the largest collection of butterflies, insects and birds' eggs – nearly 6,400 specimens – in the entire region. So it was not really surprising that by the age of fifteen he was leading a team of bird watchers on regular weekend expeditions in the Pyrenees. If a sense of adventure throbbed in his blood it was soon overshadowed by his sense of vocation for the church. He was enrolled in a seminary of the Lazarists, the order founded by St Vincent de Paul. After celebrating his ordination Mass at the Congregation de la Mission, on 5 November, 1850, he settled down to teaching and study, part of this time in north-west Italy.

His choice of religious order had another, more secular, motive. When the eighteenth-century Jesuits were suppressed in China, their work was taken over by the less academic Lazarists whom the Chinese authorities preferred for that very reason. The truth was that the young David had always nursed a secret dream to go to the Orient.

Indeed constant dreams of China followed him through troubled sleep. On 30 November, 1852 he gave rein to his feelings in a letter to his Superior-General at the rue de Sevres, Paris ... *'Although I am perfectly satisfied with my position here, I never stop dreaming at night about joining the Chinese Mission. For the past twelve years I have thought of nothing else than of working for the salvation of non-believers. It was for that reason I embraced a religious career. The twenty-seven years I have on my back would be more desirably spent helping such infidels. Since a child I have felt this to be God's calling ...'* His appeal fell on deaf ears. He was to wait ten years.

'Marco Polo's writings about China convince me that it must be alive with undiscovered treasures,' he told his father, citing the discovery of the Common Panda (*Ailuropoda microta*) by Professor Frederic Cuvier in 1825.

David's big chance came in 1862. Providentially, as he put it, ten missionaries were suddenly needed in China. When he left France to take up one of the appointments he also carried a commission from the Natural History Museum in Paris to collect specimens of fauna and flora. By the time he was well lodged in the French Legation at Beijing, he found himself also working for the French government, which had been greatly impressed by the excellence

*The first known photograph of Armand David when he was studying for the priesthood at Paris in about 1848, kindly lent by Mr Bob Edmonds his great grand-nephew.*

of his specimens sent to the museum from the south of China.

By 1865 he had catalogued over 3,000 discoveries, topped by that of the unique deer known to the Chinese as ssu-pu-hsiang (The Four Dissimilarities – neither horse, nor ox, nor reindeer nor goat), now classified as *elaphurus davidianus*, or Père David's Deer. Around this time he also spent several months beyond the Great Wall at royal Jehol, now known as Chengde, penetrated Tibet where he sang a Mass, explored the neighbouring province of Tsinghai ('Blue Sea') with an area of 432,000 sq.km and China's largest lake, the Koko'nor (5,888 sq.km), offering a super abundance of wildlife to investigate, before moving on to Mongolia for ten months. He was a powerhouse of energy and amazed his Chinese hunters.

His three expeditions, covering 35,000km, much of the time on foot, lasted from 1862 to 1874. For our purpose, it is the middle period of the second expedition, lasting four years, which is of immediate interest.

The year was 1868 and the month May. Père David had nearly six years of China under his cassock, and at forty he was still strong enough to put in a good eight-hour day walking, usually disdaining the horse his Chinese assistants provided for his use. He spoke good Mandarin as well as three dialects, and understood five others. And at all times he wore Chinese dress.

He only employed Chinese Christians and on this 27 May, with a group of hunters who rejoiced in the simple names Lin, Yuen, Han, Ho, Li, Wu, Mo and the Yang brothers, plus ten other Christian Chinese who volunteered to act as porters, he set out from the Legation Quarter at Beijing to the merry sound of firecrackers and music, which he later noted with obvious amusement in his diary. Their 300 kg baggage was carried in shoulder baskets. But before this expedition had run its full course the weight of baggage would increase to 1,620 kg, including nearly 500 species of birds – 'not a quarter to be found in Europe!' he exulted – and 110 different kinds of mammal.

On that day he wrote this: '*Mes porteurs connaiss-ent pas la route, mais ils plaisantent comme des enfants qui s'en vont en vacances!*' ('My porters don't know the route but they behave like children off on holiday!'). They moved south.

In mid-October they braved the throat of the spectacular but terrifying forty-three-kilometre Three Gorges, '*par le fleuve bleu*' (by the blue river), as he pointedly referred to the translated name Yangtze, which had been coined by Westerners (albeit that every fathom of its waters is a muddy brown). They reached a freezing Chongqing five weeks later, walked solidly for another thirty-eight days to Chengdu, and then moved into the almost impenetrable hinterland of the Sichuan Alps. Usually they lodged in cabins built into the ground and made of straw for warmth. In his diary he recorded that even the cows they encountered had their hooves bound with straw. Temperatures now plummeted to 30° below zero.

By early March of the following year, now 1869, they were carrying out a series of profitable forays in the area of Maoping, which is little over 100km south of Baoxing and located in the Laingshan Yi Autonomous Region in Sichuan. On the eleventh, as they were returning to base camp near Baoxing Xian, about 100 km from Chengdu, they were met by the owner of the Yan Jinggon valley they were crossing, Li Kaita, who cordially invited them to break their journey and stay the night at his place. In his diary Père David wrote: '*In this pagan's home I saw a large pelt of the famous black and white bear.*' (He had already heard of the creature's existence through a tutor at the Imperial Palace who said that one of the royal rooms had such a pelt for a rug – but he thought of it in terms of a black and white bear.) '*When my hunters became aware of my interest in this scientifically unique animal they assured me they would henceforth do their very best to kill me one of these carnivores.*'

Three days passed fairly uneventfully. They did, however, collect some unusual birds, including a new species of owl, a superb tragopan, some rare black voles and a large red bullfinch – '*the first of*

*The habitat of the Giant Panda is at times untamed and impenetrable.*

this new species I have seen in the area.' On 14 March he wrote: '*Fog. My hunters have brought me an enormous wild boar with tiny ears and black bristles tinged with grey tips, which I acquired for about twenty-five francs. A Chinese priest, Father Fang, a native of these parts, has helped to obtain some rare beetles which are new to me – but my hunters haven't yet caught a black and white bear!*'

The days that followed were empty, painful and depressing – they spent sleepless nights soaked to the skin in rain, they became lost for hours into the night, and some of the hunters had disappeared. Then, to cap it all, Père David received news of the death of his 'beloved' bishop at Beijing, Monseigneur Mouly, the previous 4 December. But then suddenly 23 March dawned with the excitement of his returning hunters – with a young panda, the first he had seen in its entirety.

He wrote: '*Its colours are the same as those of the adult pelt I examined the other day at Li's place. It is not merely unique because of its colours, but also on account of its hairy paws underneath and by other features.*'

The panda, '*sold to me for a rather steep price*' (twenty-five francs, according to what he later told Professor Milne-Edwards), had been killed to make its transport easier over the rough terrain. His diary gives no hint of being disturbed at this wanton killing but goes on flowingly to describe with enthusiasm the nature of numerous other species which the hunters had brought down the mountainside.

Nine days later on 1 April, the Yang brothers presented him with a large, superb-looking adult panda which, he said, '*has exactly the same colouring as the other – though not terribly clean.*' To his surprise and pleasure 3 April saw them catching, of all things, a pair of Common Pandas which had first been discovered in China nearly fifty years earlier by fellow Frenchman Frederic Cuvier. His hunters called them 'mountain children' in Chinese and explained it was because of their cries resembling those of very small children.

On 15 April the Yangs brought him another large panda, a male, they said, and then proceeded to tell

*The first Giant Panda seen by Western eyes – this one caught by the Yang brothers on April 1, 1869. Its pelt was later sent to the Paris Natural History Museum for display.*

him that the black and white bears are '*much easier to catch than the Tibetan bears. They feed themselves entirely on vegetable matter*' (presumably referring to bamboo), '*but their numbers are extremely scarce and only to be found in the higher wooded mountain slopes.*'

We know that the first and third pandas were delivered to him dead but, curiously, he makes no mention about the second which was alive when he saw it. However, we can assume it had to be put down then and there since he crated all three panda pelts and skeletons for shipment to Paris. These specimens, like some of the other rarities, were preserved in ice wrapped in straw, a system of refrigeration which the Ming had devised four centuries earlier. After intensive examination by Curator Professor Alphonse Milne-Edwards, they were stuffed and put on display in the Natural History Museum.

It has to be accepted that the missionary, albeit a devotee of St Francis, could not have been averse to killing in the first instance. Apart from the great number of specimens sent to Paris, those which were displayed in museums he established at St Lazare, Savonne and Beijing itself, all contained the 'fruits' of skilled marksmanship, very often his. A glance through the pages of his imperishable diaries reveals the familiar phrases: '*Je tue aussi un traquet cendre, je tue un joli Gobe-mouche nouveau . . . parmi les oiseaux que je tue aujourd'hui . . .*' ('I also killed an Ashen Wheatear, I killed a pretty new Flycatcher

*Père David, wearing his habitual Chinese dress, at the age of 45.*

... among the birds that I shot today ...'). The entry for 11 March of that year is in itself very revealing: '*Nous parvenons à denicher dans le creux d'un rocher une vieille guenon qu'un heureux coup de fusil a rendu morte à nos pieds*' ('We succeeded in dislodging from a rock hollow an old female monkey which a happily placed shot brought dead to our feet').

Examination of the anatomical features of the three pandas convinced him of their phylogenesis (racial history) in the animal kingdom. For him there was no question that they were members of *Ursidae*, the bear family. As they were being prepared for shipment, he included a note stating the reasons for his scientific name *Ursus Melanoleuca*. However, when the recipient, his mentor and friend Milne-Edwards, completed his own exhaustive examination of every inch of the carcasses and organs he told the missionary, on his brief return in 1870, that he was completely mistaken, that the animals were members of *Procyonidae*, the racoon family, and that he had changed their scientific name to *Ailuropoda Melanoleuca*! Before returning to China in 1872 for the third time, an undismayed David published his first notes on the pandas' habits, and sticking to his *ursus* name. Two years later Milne-Edwards published a full report on the anatomy of *Ailuropoda*.

Père David's third journey into China, lasting sixteen-and-a-half months, yielded no further pandas nor any news of them. That saga was over and done with. When chronic ill health, brought about by his years of intense deprivation and labours in China finally forced him to leave, he set sail from Shanghai on the good ship 'Sindh' on 3 April, 1874, reaching Marseilles on 15 May after a smooth voyage. He scribbled three words on the last page of his China diary, '*sauf et sain*' ('safe and sound').

Meanwhile scientists, agog at the news of this new species, came from all over the world to inspect it. Not all agreed with David or with Milne-Edwards. Arguments raged for over a century. Was the lone Père David right – or mistaken?

We shall see later how the opinions diverged up to recent years.

*The Giant Panda's closest relative ... The bear (below) or the racoon?*

# CHAPTER THREE

# Hunted!

TWENTY-NINE YEARS WERE TO PASS FROM PÈRE DAVID'S death in 1900 before the panda became headlines again. This time Theodore Roosevelt II,* son of the former President of the United States, inheriting his father's safari lust, had become the first Westerner to kill a panda. The date was 13 April, 1929. In addition, Roosevelt, who was accompanied by his brother Kermit – with whom he had an arrangement whereby they would both shoot at the same time if they sighted a panda so as to 'share the honour'† – brought back a further five panda carcasses which duly appeared in the Field Museum of Natural History in Chicago.

---

*In 1984, Mrs Nancy Reagan presented the Beijing authorities with a gift of money and two Jeeps from her Penny Panda Fund. 'Long may they live,' she said softly. Ten days later she attended the fortieth D-Day anniversary celebrations in Normandy with President Reagan. There she laid a wreath on the grave of the first US general to fall in action. He was Theodore Roosevelt II!

†During World War II, Roosevelt confided to Brigadier-General Francis Biddle, Inspector-General of the US Forces in the UK, how he had fired 'that panda shot a split second' before his brother.

Attracted by the unique black and white quarry, wealthy big-game hunters, mostly American playboys in the Gatsby mould, now converged on China to participate in this latest sport. Thirty-nine pandas were to fall to their guns over the next few years. The Chinese were powerless to act in the absence of wildlife protection laws. China's Finance Minister, T. V. Soong, is reported to have said: 'To think that some of these people were at Harvard with me!'

For one man the last straw came when Dean Sage, co-leader of an expedition sponsored by the American Museum of Natural History, shot a female panda and horrified the Chinese present by cutting off part of its rump which he cooked for breakfast over the campfire, an act which prompted the Shanghai *Evening Post*, despite its American ownership, to print a sour banner headline across the front page: PANDABURGER!

The man who found a remarkable way to atone for that callous act was Floyd Tangier Smith.

*The future Panda Man of China in his youth above, and right as a popular member of Dartmouth track team, 1904, seen at the far left of the middle row.*

# CHAPTER FOUR

# Tangier Smith

BORN AT YOKOHAMA IN 1882 OF AMERICAN MISSIONARY parents and raised with Japanese as his mother tongue, Tangier Smith bore the traditional family name to commemorate his ancestor, Colonel William Smith, who lived at Tangier in the mid-seventeenth century. He later graduated from two of America's Ivy League colleges, Dartmouth and Bowdoin, where he cut a winning figure on the running track and rifle range. Entering the world of finance, he soon found success with the International Banking Corporation, becoming a familiar figure in New York, Panama, London – where he was based with his Californian wife Elizabeth – Bombay and Hong Kong.

*Tangier Smith*

It was a chance trip across the Pearl River into China with a group of hunters that shattered the calm of his life. He found China – and hunting – irresistible. He was in his mid-forties when he announced to Elizabeth his new dream of becoming a hunter. While she remained in London, Tangier Smith joined the Shanghai firm of Gaston, Williams and Wigmore, which was known in China as 'God Wonders Why'. He captained the leading local rifle team and frequently raced a horse by the name of 'Ajax' to victory in the Shanghai Race Club's regular meetings. This life style led to increasing contacts with local big-gamers. Suddenly he quit his cosy job for the rigours of full-time hunting.

The rigours were compensated for with colourful adventures in Siberia, Indo-China, the Himalayas and Tibet where, according to the *Bowdoin Alumnus*, he was reported killed. In fact he was nursed back to health by a monk on the instructions of the thirteenth Dalai Lama.

*Pandas enjoy climbing trees. Coming down, though, is the problem, especially the last few feet when they will leap for the ground and always land with a thump!*

Back in China, Tangier Smith had the good fortune to employ a team of nine hunters with nearly 350 years combined experience, whose leader was an intrepid Han Chinese by the name of Lin Yu . . . the grandson of one of Père David's hunters! He knew the panda country like the back of his hand. Now began an eight-year-long association with the Westerner. They became very close and taught each other smatterings of their respective languages.

From 1930–2 he was leading the Marshall Field Expedition, substituting rifle for a lasso which his old friend Frank 'Bring 'Em Back Alive' Buck had taught him to use with deadly accuracy. His score was several thousand species for world zoos.

It was at this time that he had his first encounter with the Giant Panda. It happened on 19 June, 1932, at Gin Dachou in Sichuan but, as reported in the *New York Times*, the animal died some days later from unknown causes. Tangier Smith, who had taken the trouble to learn taxidermy, prepared and mounted the pelt and sent it to the Field Museum in Chicago where it joined the Roosevelt panda display.

It was small wonder that the Dean Sage episode deeply affected him. From the time he set eyes on 'the ambling beauty' of the black and white animal at Gin Dachou, pandas became the consuming passion of his life and 'pandaland' his oyster. He ventured forth five times to pry open the shell and acquire the lustrous pearl which had eluded the Westerners bent only on carnage.

Once, early in July 1935, when he reached Tianquan, about fifteen kms from Baoxing, Lin told him in hushed tones: 'We are walking over the grave of history.' He was referring to Père David and his own grandfather who had passed by there on a number of occasions sixty-five years earlier. Two days later the party ran into a company of Chinese troops heading for the Snowy Mountains. That was history too. Tangier Smith learned later from a Shanghai friend, Arthur Sowerby – editor of the *Manchu News Letter* and the top China Kennel Club judge – that the soldiers had been the Red Army's Long Marchers headed by that 'troublesome chap' Mao Zedong, eluding Chiang Kai-Shek's Nationalists!

Four of the expeditions accounted for eleven pandas skilfully noosed, using a 'luring' technique which he had devised and was later to hint at in a BBC programme about his panda adventures. But on each occasion, his luck ran out. Seven broke their bonds and two escaped. We shall see later what happened to the tenth and eleventh.

Meanwhile, a worse stroke of luck struck in November 1936. Ruth Harkness, a New York dress designer and widow of a former, short-term associate of Smith's who had recently died in the Zhongshan Hospital at Shanghai, decided to go to China and organize an expedition in memory of her husband. She flew to Chengdu, hired five local hunters, and headed north-west, unknowingly towards Tangier Smith's territory, arriving coincidentally in exactly the same area in time to hear a rumour that one of Tangier Smith's assistants had caught a panda, a baby one at that. She deliberately went to verify the story and offered the young Chinese hunter eighty dollars for the cub, an offer he was unable to resist. It was a fortune by Chinese standards. The cub's new owner thereupon called it, appropriately, 'Su-Lin' meaning 'Happy Moment'. Then she flew back to Shanghai, smuggled her treasure past the Customs without waiting to see if they would grant her an exit permit for the animal, and boarded the SS *McKinlay* with three hours to spare before sailing. She arrived without mishap in the US where the cub was rightly claimed as the first live panda seen in the West.

At the Bronx Zoo in New York her negotiations went sour. She was asking $20,000 for 'Su-Lin' which the zoo management felt was astronomical. On 27 February, 1937, she deposited the panda at Chicago's famed Brookfield Zoo for temporary safe keeping and for the next nine weeks it was cared for in the home of the zoo's director, Edward Bean, by his daughter Mary. According to her diary the panda had tripled in size to almost twenty kilograms, principally on a daily diet of two raw carrots, a half head of lettuce, three or four stalks of celery, spinach, fruit juice, vegetable soup with pabulum and cod liver oil.

On 19 April, Brookfield bought 'Su-Lin' with an $8,750 contribution towards Mrs Harkness's proposed new expedition to China. It was a good buy. 'Su-Lin' moved into new air-conditioned quarters and was displayed to the public for the first time on Sunday, 22 August, 1937. The zoo was packed with 58,524 visitors, its *biggest* daily attendance since the 58,304 on opening day in 1921.

'Su-Lin' became a national figure in the US when her picture appeared on millions of breakfast cereal packets for which the Quaker Oat Company of Chicago paid her $16,000. The blurb on the boxes described 'Su-Lin' as 'native species of Tibet'!

The following February Mrs Harkness returned from China with 'Mei-Mei', a baby brother for 'Su-Lin'. The two never met. On 28 March, 1938, 'Su-Lin' sickened and died three days later – a death recorded throughout the world in spite of an impending World War II. The public transferred its affection to 'Mei-Mei' and Brookfield Zoo smashed all attendance records that year – 2,089,223!

*The outside world had certainly heard about the mysterious Giant Pandas of China and those fortunate enough to have visited the Paris Natural History Museum had seen one of Père David's historical trio in its stuffed condition. But this was the first picture ever taken of a live panda – 'Su-Lin' in April, 1937, at Chicago's Brookfield Zoo.*

Back in China the words in Tangier Smith's diary speak for themselves: '*I may be shattered but Pao Guang-ming was certainly mortified when Lin and the others rounded on him and said that, as a member of the expedition, the panda rightly was ours and that by selling it he was insulting our joint labours. He is losing so much face over this that I guess he'll make an excuse to quit.*' Sure enough three days later Pao, unable to endure his colleagues' cold silence, disappeared. The $80 was found on a stool in Tangier Smith's tent.

Through the American media he made a big rumpus about the false claim by Mrs Harkness of bringing the first panda out of China. His threat to pursue the matter in court was in vain. He was much too involved in China. Later, however, several Americans who had been in China voiced support for his story from evidence collected in Chengdu. An Atlanta lawyer, Richard Reynolds III, went so far as to claim he had proof of the validity of Tangier Smith's right to ownership of the cub.

The greatest blow was yet to befall him. That was panda number eleven.

*Floyd Tangier Smith with Chang on the first leg of his long journey to London in August, 1937.*

Months after this unpleasant episode, on 21 June, 1937 to be precise, Tangier Smith fulfilled his dream. He caught a large male panda, which he estimated to be about 110 lb (50 kg) and in such superb condition that he named it 'Chang', which means 'Strong'. 'He's the finest specimen I've ever seen!' he exulted. *The China Year Book 1939* recorded that ten days later he caught a second, presumably in poor condition because it died within forty-eight hours for no apparent reason.

Having been photographed with 'Chang', he reached Chengdu in time to 'hitch' a ride in a military plane going to Shanghai. As they rose above the clouds the pilot, Captain Gao Sun-li, broke the terrible news to him. Japan had that morning invaded Nanking, the capital. The date was 7 July, one not to be forgotten by the Chinese for many a long year.

At Shanghai, Randall Gould, editor of the *Evening Post*, reported the scene on the city's river-front Bund two days later: '*An estimated 25,000 Westerners and robed Chinese, not to mention 500 children from the American School, whose screams of delight failed to put off the black and white prince, thronged the street to watch His Furry Highness amble aboard the ship that was to take him to Merry England! What a sight to take our minds off the Jap occupation of the capital!*'

Had Tangier Smith not caught that ship but waited for the next sailing, the outcome of this story might have proved very different. On 14 August, by which time he was nearing the Mediterranean, a lone Japanese plane dropped four bombs on overcrowded Shanghai killing or wounding 1,600 people in three minutes – in the district where he had rented a villa.

Days later the ship ran into the tail end of a typhoon. Poor 'Chang' could not take the mountainous seas. Prolonged sickness brought death within twenty-four hours. His body was consigned to the deep of the South China Sea.

# How to Catch a Panda

In his October 1937 broadcast, Tangier Smith said:

*'The greatest problem in catching pandas is to find the right kind of bait to lure them. Bamboo is out of the question because there is so much of it at hand. But I have evolved a lure which succeeds every time. I don't believe one can capture a live panda by any other means. For the time being I shall keep this secret to myself until I return with pandas as proof positive!'*

Nearly fifty years were to pass before the secret was revealed to the author by Lin Yu's sole surviving daughter in the People's Hotel at Chongqing. She said:

*'My father told us that each time the foreigner Tangier Smith would arrive from Shanghai his stores included three sacks of cubed sugar. He would place several of the cubes within the noose of a lassoo which was spread out on the ground, and then distribute other pieces of sugar among the nearby bamboo thickets. This, he explained the first time it was done, was to attract the pandas' attention seeing they were unable to resist anything with a sweet taste. Having once scented and consumed the first piece of sugar they would go to the next and then the next until they were well in the noose. From a hidden position the rope would be pulled taut. As it snarled the panda's feet a second lasso, cast by Tangier Smith, would encircle its shoulders while the rest of the party would dash out from their hiding places to secure the captive. There were times when the pandas got away, but generally speaking it was a successful method. Everyone was sworn to secrecy about it. As devout Buddhists they could not break their vow ...'*

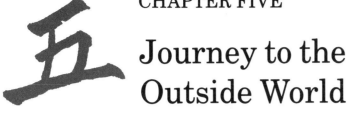

# CHAPTER FIVE

# Journey to the Outside World

IF THE PRIVATIONS OF CLIMATE, TERRAIN, BAD FOOD and lack of sleep took their toll on Père David, they were exacting a sterner penalty on the American hunter, now suffering painfully with his weak lungs. Tangier Smith was down from 79 kg to a mere 57 kg, there was a stoop to his beanpole figure and no longer did the lean, bearded features resemble those of a professor of Classics, but more a sick tramp. Shocked by his appearance at Tilbury, Elizabeth insisted on his seeing a doctor. On Monday, 27 September, a Harley Street specialist warned him bluntly: 'One more trip to China and you're a goner!' He was in the advanced stages of tuberculosis.

To Elizabeth's dismay and the astonishment of his local circle of friends he made a broadcast for a BBC Radio programme *The World Goes By* two weeks later on Wednesday, 6 October, when he described his panda adventures, admitted his 'lousy' bad luck but added defiantly: 'I'm going back to China for bigger and better pandas. This time they shan't escape or die on me!'

A rumour leaked out that the Zoological Society of London was behind this plan and brought letters of protest to the Press alleging that the methods of trapping were cruel. W. P. Pyecraft, FZS, a well-known naturalist, came to Smith's rescue in the *Illustrated London News* by writing: '*This criticism is ill-informed for, naturally, every possible care is taken to ensure that no cruelty shall attend their capture. Cruelty, in any case, would render the chances of their reaching us alive extremely small!*'

Tangier Smith was no fool, despite the seemingly

foolhardy risks he took. He realized that a long rest was essential. With Elizabeth he took a flat at Sussex Square in Brighton for six months. They became familiar figures on the seashore and the famous pier, and made friends with a celebrity neighbour, the French actress Yvonne Arnaud. The second of May saw them both China-bound, for this time Elizabeth insisted on going, too — in spite of the Shanghai bombing which might be repeated since the political situation in China was rapidly deteriorating. She stayed with the US Consul-General and his wife, while Tangier Smith headed up the Yangtze for his familiar hunting grounds to be reunited with his old assistant, Lin, and a team of Chinese helpers.

Lin broke the news that missionaries at St Michael's in Chengdu had reported panda sightings at a favourite watering place of theirs near one of the missionary schools in the Cao Po (Grassy Slope) district about 100 kilometres north-west of Chengdu, in a valley completely surrounded by high mountains. Without losing a moment, the party headed in that direction, establishing the usual collecting posts as they went. Had they but known, such preliminaries were to prove a complete waste of time.

It was mid-August. The yellow eye of the sun blazed relentlessly, never below 40°C (105°F). They settled down for the long wait near the place where one of the missionaries led them, this being the technique for catching pandas so sensitive to human activity that they disappeared at the sound of a snapped twig.

The incredible happened. Tangier Smith caught five pandas in two days and on the third a small cub waddled straight into his arms. He was cock-a-hoop. Six pandas. *Six!* Such a thing had never been known. Not SIX LIVE ONES!

Lin, on the other hand, felt uneasy. Aware that Tangier Smith planned to take the pandas to England, fresh doubts gnawed in his mind. How would it be possible? England — the other side of the world!

Lin was no run-of-the-mill hunter. He came from a long line of time-tried experts. Had not his own

36

grandfather, Lin Wang, been with Père David's famous expedition and brought him one of the historic pandas? Now, emboldened by their tie of friendship over the years, he reminded Tangier Smith of the panda's prodigious daily intake of bamboo for its survival. 'They need so much, perhaps three or four hundred stems a day – or more. They never stop eating! Your journey will take weeks. So the animals will surely die. There are *six* to be fed!'

Tangier Smith felt a fist of fear inside. He recognized the sense of Lin's words but remained silent. That night, 16 August, he wrote in his diary: '*I have to put on a bold front. The others must never suspect that I have perhaps bitten off more than I can chew (let alone what the pandas can chew!). I have a faint glimmer of a plan and propose walking into the forest at dawn to think . . .*'

He rose at five and disappeared into the green silence for three hours. When he returned there was a confidence in his bearing and Lin, as he would later say, knew that 'he was up to something'.

When Tangier Smith outlined his plan, Lin Yu was aghast. How was it humanly possible to transport a mountain of bamboo fodder, which his master seemed to be suggesting? Such an undertaking was too formidable even to contemplate. It was fraught with obstacles. The outcome could only mean total disaster. He had not reckoned with the other's deep-seated determination. Now as Tangier Smith quietly but firmly detailed stage by stage what he had in mind, sketching a rough map and producing figures, it suddenly flowered with possibility.

He began by pointing out their main advantage – had Lin overlooked it? – that five of the animals were on the small side, the smallest, in fact, no more than about 18 kg at the very most. The sixth was perhaps half a full-sized panda.

'*On the accepted basis,*' he went on, '*that a six-foot, 300-pounder* (a 1·8-m animal weighing 140 kg) *consumes the amount you say it does, 400 stems of cane, I calculate that their combined daily feed should not exceed more than a fifth of what six large pandas would eat – in other words, 600 stems a day.*

'It will take about three weeks to reach Chongqing, ten days down the Yangtze to Shanghai, and a month for the voyage to England. Which makes about, say, nine. We shall therefore need about 37,000 pieces of bamboo with a bit extra for any problems we may run into.'

Lin would later describe the hunter's cool, matter-of-fact air as he recited the startling figures which, he knew only too well, spelled the pandas' life-line. The confidence he displayed, however, proved contagious. The team now felt no lingering doubts about their ability to pull it off. They sensed that a new page of wildlife history was about to be written – and wanted to be part of it!

A mammoth operation was put into action, the men toiling for eight days, from dawn to dusk, hacking, cutting, trimming and bundling the small canes, small because Tangier Smith was aware of the pandas' selectivity in their choice of fodder, disdaining most of the canes except for the centre portion, presumably for flavour and nutrition. Gradually hillocks of cut bamboo appeared over a wide area.

*The Incredible Journey starring Floyd Tangier Smith and six pandas. Was it any wonder that the young Zhou Enlai called it 'Six Panda Madness'.*

Route taken by Floyd Tangier Smith in 1938

0          400km.

0          200 miles

While only incidental to the Great Panda operation, the hunters somehow found time in between this fever of activity to catch other species, twenty-seven in all, including a superb young golden monkey. They were added to the panda circus.

Tangier Smith's diary entry for Thursday, 17 September read: *'The scene is one of green chaos all around us, but in a slow kind of way the plan is steadily taking shape. The men seem cheerful about it.'*

Finally, the plan firmed with the purchase of forty-two mules from local peasants. At first they were reluctant to part with their precious animals of burden, but Tangier Smith's assurance that, when he reached the embarkation point at Chongqing his hunters – who would be returning to Chengdu anyway – would bring the mules back, did the trick. That way they would make a handsome profit! Each mule was loaded with tightly compressed bundles of some one thousand canes with the balance stored in the two horse-drawn caravans used for carrying hunting equipment and supplies.

*Tangier Smith calculated that his six pandas would need 600 stems of bamboo for each day of their nine-week journey.*

A warm day on 18 September saw them break camp and head back to Chengdu, a two- or three-day trek. Then, like a bolt from the blue, *'an incredible miracle crossed our path . . .'* Two more pandas were bagged – an operation taking less than twenty minutes as the pandas were sleeping. Tangier Smith wrote: *'If six is a record, eight must surely be unbeatable!'*

As the serpentine procession swayed into the provincial capital, known for the past two thousand years as 'the storehouse of Heaven', due to its prosperity, the entire city, tipped off by the grapevine from Cao Po – which Tangier Smith called the 'bamboo telegraph' – turned out for the sight of a lifetime. Few had ever seen a Giant Panda!

The streets were gaily festooned with twenty thousand elaborately designed lanterns, normally earmarked for the annual Lunar New Year Lantern Festival dating back 1,325 years. There were great manifestations of religious fervour . . . the air, echoing with the chant of Buddhist hymns and the repeated litany *Amn mani padme hum* – 'O jewel in the lotus', was heavy with clouds of incense. Pandas were still held to be semi-deities.

All this came as no great surprise to Tangier Smith who was well aware of their superstitious beliefs. As he observed the familiar panda door gods which never failed to fascinate him, he recalled Du Fu's words of 1,200 years before about their power in driving away evil spirits ... yet this was the twentieth century!

Crying out in Sichuan dialect picked up from Lin, 'Stand back for the holy pandas!' he led the incredible procession to the town hall and presented an astonished mayor with their latest catch – the pair becoming the first pandas exhibited in their own country! Before setting out south for Chongqing, he staged a mock christening ceremony 'annointing' each animal with green tea and having it weighed. The details he recorded were:

| | |
|---|---|
| *Ming* | 15.3 kg |
| *Chang* | 41 kg |
| *Tang* | 63 kg |
| *Sung* | 62.2 kg |
| *Grandma* | 63 kg |
| *Happy* | 100.5 kg |

The last two were not, after all, named after past dynasties like the other four. Tangier Smith had learned from Lin that his grandmother, a Chengdu woman, was that day celebrating her eighty-eighth birthday. An exultant Tangier Smith quipped: 'We shall honour your dear grandma and make her happy!' Hence the names 'Grandma' and 'Happy'.

A telegraph message was sent to Elizabeth. *'Reserve passages for England – also for six pandas. Allow five weeks.'*

For the next twenty-four days they trekked the 582-kilometre road to Chongqing in the absence of any railroad. Gruelling. Tortuous. Primitive. Pitted with holes and gaps at every step. Small wonder the great Du Fu had also once written: *'The road into Heaven is easier to travel than the roads of Sichuan ...'*

It was during this part of their journey that Tangier Smith's relations with the pandas blossomed emotionally, almost like those of a closely knit family. His diary reveals the bond he felt and how a deep sense of responsibility welled inside him.

He described the routine of his days, sometimes in a coolie chair, but more often on foot to show his willingness to share the rigours of the road under a broiling sun:

'Semi-divine or not, they most certainly exert a profound effect upon me. I consider their welfare at all times, watching anxiously if they are eating and exactly how much, making quite certain that they consume enough water and always looking out for more streams, dreading the hour our own canteen supplies may run dry and there is none at hand to draw. I find myself even fretting if they fail to defecate with regularity. They have become the children of my life, the children I never had. In return, I believe, and even feel it strongly at times, that they look upon me as their father figure. Or should it be mother! Nothing has so enriched my life as their close presence. They have, in fact, hypnotized my will to succeed . . .'

*Tangier Smith with one of his 'children': 'I sat for two-and-a-half hours watching "Chang" consume 118 stems of bamboo without a stop. Then he dropped flat out and slept for two hours. I now realised the enormity of the problem of feeding them if I was ever to reach London Zoo with them alive and well!'*

Progress was hampered by the pandas being allowed to cool off in local rivers or streams and by Tangier Smith's insistence on having them regularly exercised on their leads fashioned out of six-metre lengths of rope, as a break from the cages which had been made for them and carried in the stores. They entered the sweltering mountain-ringed city of Chongqing on 16 October amidst even greater tumult and mass hysteria than before. Professor Han Feng-wu, a boy of twelve at the time, recalls the scene to this day:

'By a stroke of good fortune it was a Sunday when they appeared and most people were off. We, who had never before seen a panda other than in our picture books, could scarcely believe our eyes! The sight of five padding meekly alongside their keepers, who held on to their collars, was only surpassed by the *appearance of the tall, very thin foreigner who carried a small panda in his arms, talking to it gently as if to distract it from the storm of excitement all around. IT WAS UNFORGETTABLE!'*

Three words also came from a young Zhou Enlai, commander of the Eighth Route Army, who witnessed the circus-like scene as it snailed past his cottage HQ at nearby Hong Yan-cun (Red Crag Village). His companions saw him shake his head. 'Six Panda Madness,' he murmured. On visiting the Beijing Zoo in 1952 to see its first pandas, he recalled the occasion. 'It was a truly remarkable performance that only a foreigner would have dared to attempt,' he said, with the ghost of a smile in his eyes.

*A rare scene – three pandas together having a good gossip, though two are mother and cub.*

# CHAPTER SIX

# Pandas at Sea

*Fascination with the ever-so-tasty bamboo!*

AN UNEXPECTED SURPRISE AWAITED TANGIER SMITH on the sun-dappled landing stage which jutted out to 'Double Jubilation', the Chinese name for the confluence of the Great River, Son of the Ocean (the Yangtze), and the Jialing. It was Elizabeth! He could hardly believe his eyes. Nor could she, never having set eyes on a Giant Panda in her life . . . and here were six!

She had flown up from Shanghai in Victor Sassoon's De Havilland Moth to warn him of the days-old Japanese occupation of the entire Yangtze Valley and the city of Wuhan which commanded the river nearly 2,240 kilometres downstream. This meant that his planned short-cut to the sea – and a ship for England – was blocked. The river-boat service was now suspended.

At first Tangier Smith attempted to shrug it off. 'You forget that my passport shows that I was born in Japan,' he said laughingly. 'Nor have I forgotten my Japanese mother-tongue. The Japanese will be only too delighted to . . .'

Elizabeth would have none of it. With presence of mind she had already arranged his escape route – a lift all the way to Canton with a convoy of trucks and cars due to leave the next morning to collect medical supplies for the Chinese Army. And Canton was on Hong Kong's doorstep, which meant the chance of a ship to England.

Tangier Smith was only too aware that this considerably longer overland route would upset his carefully thought out rationing plans. Moving south they would almost certainly find no bamboo growing on the way. But he knew that there was no other way out of this dilemma.

He took his farewell of Lin who tried to bolster his spirits by reminding him that the name Chongqing meant 'Repeated Luck' and, what was even more significant, that it was the Year of the Tiger, symbol of passion, daring – and success! All the omens were propitious, he said.

The early dawn of 16 October saw them leave the city before crowds could gather and impede their departure. They were to be on one of the most tortuous roads in south-east China for twenty-nine days, the 2,560-km journey (compared with 2,040 km by rail today) taking them through five provinces and 138 towns. Misfortune beset them almost daily and made speedier headway impossible.

The Chinese leader, Generalissimo Chiang Kai-shek, had the foresight to establish a chain of nineteen fuel depots between Chongqing – now the new capital for his united front with Mao's Red Army against the common enemy, Japan – and Canton to guarantee his supplies from Hong Kong; they nevertheless ran out of fuel several times and walked for hours, once taking a whole day, to the nearest town to hire transport, then having to wait further agonizing hours for petrol to be brought back to the convoy. There were nine blowouts. Near impassable roads were often blocked by cliff-slides and had to be painfully hand-cleared. On five occasions they were held up by mountain bandits, their lives saved only when the superstitious miscreants saw the pandas and took to their horses. They were forced to shelter in forests to avoid Japanese planes spotting their prominent Red Cross insignia all over the trucks. Twice in open country they were strafed. The pandas, in two trucks, were terrified by the thunder of low-flying aircraft and the chatter of gun-fire. They bleated for hours and, as Tangier Smith observed, went off their food for the same period.

Real disaster struck when they reached Li-seh in Kwangtung Province. The brakes of the lead truck gave as it was making a steep descent towards a narrow double-bend where it overturned and burst into flames. The pandas were safely elsewhere, but thirty-seven bundles of precious bamboo were devoured by flames, the road was blocked for eleven hours and the driver, Larry Beaton, sustained a leg injury.

Compensating for this major set-back the next town, Shao-Kuan, proved to be a mere twenty-four kilometres away and, in no time, the injured man was in the care of a local woman whose knowledge of Xi Yi – Chinese herbal medicine – proved sound. After an enforced stay of only three days – during which peasants from far and wide came to enjoy a grandstand view of the black and white sextet – they moved on. After crossing the Pearl River Delta for Hong Kong they reached Holt's Wharf on 14 November, with barely thirty-six hours before the Blue Funnel 11,000-tonne S S *Antenor* was due to sail for London.* It provided them with enough time to see the pandas comfortably settled in their new surroundings and then speed off to the markets of shoreside Kowloon to search for supplementary stores now urgently needed. They were able to lay their hands on seven hundred eggs, two sacks of milk powder, half a tonne of apples and some nuts.

'In my all years of seagoing,' Captain G. R. Leslie said later, 'there was never a voyage like it. One of the pandas died from seasickness during a storm off Sumatra. From then it was smooth sailing most of the way. The animals were walked round the decks exactly a hundred times a day for exercise. Oh, what a sight!'

The exhausted Tangier Smith, now deeply affected

---

*Had Tangier Smith succeeded in taking the short-cut route down the Yangtze to Shanghai, it would not have got him to London any earlier. He would have found that the only UK-bound ship had already sailed on 15 October, when he was a day out of Chongqing. Oddly, the ship was in fact the *Antenor* and heading for Yokohama – his birthplace. On 23 October it left for Kobe and reached Hong Kong on 14 November – in the nick of time for a passage – otherwise he would have been stranded in China for seventeen more days, the next sailing to England. The pandas would surely have died.

*A cub has his very first climb.*

*Pandas are ever curious.*

by 'Chang's' death, his second panda of that name lost at sea in two years running, kept to his quarters for the rest of the voyage. The panda's death, however, proved a blessing in disguise for the others by providing them with an increase in rations from the rapidly diminishing supply. However, it was still necessary for Elizabeth to make urgent forays for dribbles of supplementary fodder in the markets at Singapore (23 November), Colombo (30 November), and Suez (10 December) – not only for the pandas but also for the rest of the collection. But by the time they had passed Gibraltar on 18 December, the pandas, desperate for roughage to counter the amount of meat being provided by the ship's butcher (on Tangier Smith's instructions) to eke out the extras Elizabeth had bought, were clawing furiously at the woodwork of their cages as a substitute for bamboo. Now it was touch and go for survival; a drama that drained Tangier Smith of most of his remaining strength.

According to the Blue Funnel *Bulletin*, the cages collapsed under this onslaught: '*The only alternative then was to empty and clean out the potato lockers which were also on the poop – and so they became home to the pandas for the last few days. Given time, they would have met the same fate as the cages.*'

By the strangest irony, the pandas, originating from a snowy habitat, reached a Britain blanketed with snow for over a week! Tilbury on 23 December was hardly visible in a fresh blizzard. Three hours after docking, the furry five were bolting down creamy rice gruel, rusks, fruit and vitamin supplements provided by welcoming officials from London Zoo. The rest of the collection was cared for, too, but the golden monkey was shortly to die.

An amusing interlude followed. The zoo authorities had brought large cages, each in turn being landed on the poop to take a panda. The pandas, however, were having none of it. They could smell the previous occupants and backed away resolutely – 'Grandma' sat on her haunches blocking the cage entrance for twenty-five minutes! A push by Elizabeth '*only made her rear up on her hind legs and turn round, swinging her arms, which caused the*

*lightning disappearance of all the advising spec-*
*tators, most of whom did not wait to get off the poop*
*in the normal manner!'* reported the *Bulletin*.

What marvellous TV footage that scene would
have made. Had their arrival taken place today, the
quay would have been swamped with film crews,
photographers and reporters. None of the media
turned up, although *The Times*, tipped off by a
phone call, ran a three-decker headline.

In the long article that followed (which was fair
coverage in a newspaper filled with news about Hitler, Santa Claus and snow-bound Britain), the successful hunter was described, to his irritation, as Mr
Floyd-Smith. Oddly, his name, Tangier, featured in
a headline on the next page – but referred to a
political scandal in Tangier itself!

Christmas Day saw the pandas installed at the
zoo's quarantine quarters where the scales yielded
the surprise that, in spite of their ninety-five-day
ordeal, they had actually put on weight. 'Ming' was
now 25.4 kg, 'Tang' and 'Sung' both 68.1 kg,
'Grandma' 72.6 kg and 'Happy' 106.96 kg.

*The five pandas arrived in
Britain to find it covered
with familiar snow.*

# CHAPTER SEVEN

# The Gentle Hunter

*Fockelmann's letter to Tangier Smith which decided the future of the two pandas 'Happy' and 'Grandma'. Tangier Smith was often referred to as 'Major', even in Brompton Hospital records and the lease of his apartment at Brighton, but neither the United States nor British military authorities have any record of service in the Armed Forces.*

TOO ILL TO GO TO THEIR MAYFAIR FLAT WHERE THE absence of any help would prove a burden to Elizabeth, the hunter decided they should move into the Imperial Hotel at Russell Square. Bad news came within twenty-four hours. The London Zoo wished to keep only the three smaller pandas. So what to do with 'Grandma' and the hefty 'Happy'? What other zoos would want to buy pandas with Europe on the brink of war?

Tangier Smith contacted a business acquaintance of long standing to whom he had sold numerous species, Otto Fockelmann, director of a German firm of animal dealers, Ruhe & Fockelmann, at his London office. A deal was made and on 28 December Fockelmann wrote to Tangier Smith as follows:

*'We are prepared to take over the two large Pandas for the period whilst they are in Europe, to exhibit them to the best advantage and under the most suitable conditions. To use the animals whenever possible for useful propaganda and for the furtherance of the knowledge of these animals to the benefit of science and the general public. The Pandas will remain your property until you make arrangements with us for their sale . . .'*

Under the arrangement, Tangier Smith would receive fifty-five per cent of all 'gross monies', Fockelmann's company would pay for transport, feeding and publicity and retain the balance. They would also undertake to deliver the pandas free of charge to New York for showing at the World's Fair.

Up to now Tangier Smith had been well compensated for his latest panda enterprise. The London Zoo had paid nearly £4,000 for their trio. He also knew that he stood to make a tidy sum when the remaining pair appeared at the World's Fair in New York. In addition, seven leading manufacturers, no doubt recalling the Quaker Oats 'Su-Lin' promotion, had started making overtures from the moment an American radio network had broadcast the news of their arrival at Marseilles on 15 December. He also now had reason to believe that the New York Zoological Society was interested in acquiring the pandas after the Fair.

But 'Grandma' was not fated to share the future with 'Happy'. She died on 9 January – and by a cruel twist of fate. Having survived a land and sea journey of over 16,000 km, she went down with severe digestive trouble caused by the amount of wood gnawed from her cage on board the *Antenor* in the final days of that voyage.

Perhaps it was this last blow that proved to be too much for Tangier Smith. The dark star in his story rose three days later when, in bad shape, he was rushed to Brompton Hospital. It was too late, and little could be done for him. Discharged on 17 March, he and Elizabeth paid an anonymous visit to Whipsnade Zoo to bid an emotional farewell to their panda friends.

The couple caught the next sailing of the *Queen Mary* to New York. Nearly three months later the doyen of big-game hunting in China died at his sister's home at Mastick, Long Island, on 12 July, at the age of fifty-eight.

By the time the news trickled into China, the few English newspapers were filled with news of the British and French declaration of war on Germany – but nonetheless found space on their front pages to pay tribute to 'the Panda Man of China'. At the select Shanghai Club a commemoration lunch was hosted by Sir Victor Sassoon for 270 members and their wives, breaking the no-women rule for the first time in the club's history. Sassoon raised his glass. 'To dear old Floyd . . . the Gentle Hunter!'

At the British Embassy, now transferred to Shanghai, the flag was lowered for the first time as were the flags of six other nationalities of club members. It was the end of a special era.

Never again would the Giant Panda be hunted in China by Westerners.

Giant panda with two pawfuls of bamboo shoots as happy as a child with two lollipops.

*Sunday 26, June 1939. 'Happy', one of Tangier Smith's panda troupe, makes his American debut before 22,000 people at the St Louis Zoo. Like any normal panda, 'Happy' was far more interested in eating than posing or performing.*

# PART II

# PRESENT-DAY PANDAS ...AND THEIR ENEMIES

# CHAPTER EIGHT

# At Home in China

FOLLOWING THE VICTORIOUS REVOLUTION IN 1949 THE new government, recalling the results of Western expeditions, also heeded a warning given three years earlier when the Hong Kong newspaper *Ta Kung Pao* (whose proprietor was a far-seeing conservationist) ran a dramatic front-page banner headline which screamed its warning, the first given to the world: PANDA IN DANGER OF EXTINCTION! The story which followed presented an in-depth report from Chinese scientists who disturbingly confirmed that the animal's habitat was shrinking at an alarming rate.

The Chinese government awarded the Giant Panda the very special status of a 'National Treasure', fully protected by law.*

Henceforth panda hunting was outlawed. Even China's own zoos, wishing to acquire pandas for public display or scientific re†earch, were, and are to this day, obliged to make application to the Wildlife Ministry.

Exports were banned. Years later when it was decided to present pandas to other countries as 'messengers of friendship', the law was amended to allow only two to leave China in the same year.

At long last the Giant Panda was safe.

But . . . was it?

Fresh and extensive field studies, this time on an

---

*The Constitution says: 'Henceforth this rare and precious animal is deemed for all time a protected species.'

official level and enjoying the highest priorities, had yielded an alarming catalogue of hitherto unsuspected perils which, over the span of centuries, and in particular our own, had finally caught up with the innocent, unsuspecting victims and accounted for rapidly diminishing numbers. These perils were now fully exposed to the Chinese nation and an outside sympathetic, concerned world, for the first time. One had only to study them to realize why a crisis was imminent.

The panda's mortal enemies are:

1 STARVATION

2 POACHERS

3 BREEDING PROBLEMS

4 FIRE

5 PREDATORS

6 DEADLY DISEASE

7 HUMAN ENCROACHMENT AND THE DESTRUCTION
   OF HABITAT

These enemies are common to all five places where the panda lives. These are: Shaanxi's Qinling Mountains, the Min Shan, Qionglai and Liangshan Mountains in Sichuan and in southern Gansu Province, with middle-altitude zones enjoying a mild climate and lush vegetation.

We know that the Giant Panda originated as a carnivore, that owing to the absence of predatory instincts in its psychological make-up, it gradually developed as a herbivore, becoming the only species to effect a successful switchover from an all-meat diet – but this created a cruel paradox which has dominated its life ever since. Bamboo became its life-line. Without a prodigious daily intake, prodigious because of the plant's low nutrient, the animal will perish. There is no substitute food that can sustain it in the wild. Sometimes it will eat meat, proved by the presence of small bones found in autopsied bodies. But bamboo is a must every time.

As a former carnivore, it has inherited a short gut which prevents the breaking down of the tough bamboo cellulose passing into its stomach. A further complication is the lack of high-crowned back teeth for proper mastication, making it impossible to digest more than ten to twenty per cent of its food. This accounts for an output of large fibrous droppings which concerns everyone involved in panda work. What, then, does the panda live on? Let us examine the bamboo problem, for problem it certainly is.

*Droppings like these are passed at the rate of 8–9 kilos a day. Another legacy from its time as a carnivore is the absence of special enzymes which herbivores secrete in their organs and which help to digest coarse plant fibres. Note the undigested fibres which take five to eight hours to pass through the system!*

# CHAPTER NINE

九

# The Bamboo Death

FAR FROM THERE BEING A WORLD SHORTAGE OF BAMBOO there are about 1,200 varieties, from some fifty-five *genera*, of which one-fourth grows in China, which has about fifty million *mu* (3.4 million hectares) growing principally along the Zhujiang River in South China and in other areas south of the Changjiang River. Not more than twenty of these varieties are known to be acceptable to pandas in zoos, but those in the wild have a passion for just two distinctive kinds, which obviously contain both nutrient and flavour.

These are 'cold arrow' (*Sigarundinarea fangiana*) and 'walking stick' (*Thamnacalmus spathaceus*).* The pandas seek the former in elevations from 2,300 metres to 3,800 metres which is the limit and above which nothing grows except shrubs and grasses, and in spring descend to lower grounds to feed on the young succulent shoots of the latter. The shoots, too, of *Fargecia spathaces* – named in honour of its discoverer, the Abbé Paul Guillaume Farges at Ta-Pa Shan about the time of Waterloo – are also a favourite food.

But in all these bamboos, which belong to the same family as maize and wheat (i.e. *gnamineāe*), the fibrous quality of nutrient is low and accounts for the panda's prodigious appetite and the need to spend twelve to fourteen hours a day eating, during which it may consume four to five hundred stems.

---

*Europe was the last Continent to grow bamboo – first introduced in 1827.

*Fresh, well-grown bamboo up to 3 metres high, and ready for eating.*

When switching to the lower elevations in the spring it can consume up to six or seven hundred because the young shoots consist of mostly water.

The panda has only one stomach with intestines less than ten metres long, whereas the equally herbivorous cow, with its four-chambered stomach, has intestines more than twenty times the length of its body! During the course of a day the panda will pass about eight to nine kilos of droppings, often during the process of eating or walking. Most of these droppings contain large quantities of undigested bamboo branches and leaves which only serve to confirm that their digestive systems are not as well developed as those of other herbivores. With hindsight, Tangier Smith had every reason to be mystified about his pandas' voracity and toilet! Two days after his BBC broadcast he told a meeting of London Zoo vets: 'I am at a loss to understand what keeps the panda going. Its droppings consist almost entirely of fibre and are entirely different from herbivorous cattle. What is consumed mostly passes clean through the system. So where does the panda get its strength from?'

These types of bamboo are blighted by a mysterious cessation of growth called the 'menopause', which follows a sudden flowering and is unique among flowering plants. The result seems almost like a conspiracy of nature to imperil the panda at any cost . . .

Due to a clock-like mechanism in the plant's cell, blossom appears any time between fifty and one hundred years depending on prevailing conditions. According to Dr Thomas Soderstrom, Curator of Botany at the Smithsonian Institute at Washington DC, and a world authority on bamboo, and a number of Chinese scientists, some flowering may not even occur until 120 years after the last one, a cyclic process which to this day still baffles world scientists.

Flowering is the phenomenal thing about bamboo. Astonishingly, all plants of the same species blossom simultaneously. When a certain species blossoms, say, at Wolong, it will be going on at the same time somewhere in Europe and Africa. In its final hours of life it will seed, but years will pass before the seed grows into fresh, edible bamboo – if it has escaped hungry birds and rodents!

In China this is called the 'blossom of death', for as the beautiful gold and violet flowers wither, so do they scatter their seed. All too often, large expanses of bamboo consist of only one clone. In such cases the deadly blossom lives up to its name. It is the time Chinese botanists dread because it heralds approaching danger – the danger of a wilderness barren of food. It can be summed up in a word – famine – a famine which may last for up to fifteen years.

With the bamboo lifeless and its myriad of seed scattered throughout the forests, a relentless time-table now exerts a power that nothing can halt, and is as follows:

1  Seed takes two to three years to germinate.

2  A further four to five years before new shoots reach a height of several centimetres – and useless as food.

3  After six or seven more years the plants reach 3–3.5 metre maturity – and nutrition.*

Cold-arrow bamboo grows less high, so that the famine gap is reduced by three or four years. This snail-like rate of growth means that from the time of its 'blossom of death', the innocent and unsuspecting panda faces an empty larder which its instincts fail to anticipate. Even so, pandas are sedentary by habit, never migratory, and keep to a home base of about eight square kilometres; it would

---

*Conversely, there is a bamboo which grows in the South of France which can be 'seen' growing, at a rate of 1¼ metres in a day.

Cold arrow grows less high but fate has ordained that it takes twenty years to grow a mere two metres! The Sichuan Forestry Research Institute, which has a station in the Wanglang Nature Reserve of some 277 km, is now experimenting to speed up the growth of arrow by shortening its twenty-year growth down to five or ten years.

*Deceptive beauty. Soon this bamboo will flower itself to death, leving behind a wilderness of dead plants and an empty larder for perhaps fifteen years.*

*Sir Peter Scott inspects a specimen of cold-arrow bamboo.*

never occur to them to move on and seek fresh pastures. The barren area can be so vast that it finds itself trapped. It could never hope to survive on its supplementary pleasures which include wild fruit and flowers, birds' eggs, honey from raided hives, the bark of certain trees, rush reeds and small rodents like bamboo rats.

There have been several minor disasters when dead, starved pandas have been found, but nothing ever matched the horrific discovery of 147* dead pandas in certain parts of Gansu and Sichuan in the spring of 1976. Forestry workers were stunned by the sight of black and white carcasses littering a wilderness of dead bamboo for several kilometres around. Hundreds of rescue squads combed the mountains for starving pandas and fed them, and when the animals had regained their health they were returned to the forests. These timely measures prevented what might have become an even worse disaster.

The Cultural Revolution, which outlawed all forms of contact with the West, was responsible for keeping the outside world in ignorance of this tragedy at the time. In any event, it is doubtful if the Gang of Four and their Maoist apostles were greatly concerned with what they would have looked upon as mere panda trivia. Visiting a certain zoo on one occasion Mao's wife, Jiang Qing, stood before the pandas' enclosure and watched them dozing in the hot sun. After a moment she made the bland comment: 'Why do people make such a fuss over these creatures. They're not very entertaining, are they? And very likely expensive to keep!'

With her overthrow and a resumption of normality, the new government set up an inquiry. Their worst fears were confirmed; those very forests of

---

*Conflicting figures have ranged from 121 to 149 (ours is from an official source) but what is certain is that sixty-four were found dead in Pingwu County alone. Can you imagine it – sixty-four precious pandas, many strewn around within sight of each other! One group of farm workers mourned for weeks. 'Sleep was impossible – it was as if we had lost our own children!' they said.

death had been barren nearly a hundred years before. So if the growth rate of the bamboo in that area is true to form, there will be no fresh food available there until 1991!

An *éminence grise* of the Institute of Zoology at the Academia Sinica said: 'I believe the 1976 disaster accounted for many more pandas in the higher regions where searches were made quite impossible by heavy snow drifts capable of concealing many more bodies. In 1983, which was bad enough, we were far more prepared.'

Another scientist, however, expressed himself even more trenchantly to Dr Soderstrom when he visited Beijing in 1979. 'It is fairly certain,' he told the American botanist, 'that half the entire population was wiped out in 1976!'

This brings us to the question of just how many pandas there are in these bamboo forests. Many Chinese experts believe the number to be nearer 300–400 than the World Wildlife Fund's estimated 1,000 for which there is no firm basis, nor eye-

*Among the wilderness of dead bamboo, these young fresh green shoots, will provide no nutrition for at least another ten years.*

*Professor Hu Jin Chu (in blue), one of China's leading biologists knows these forests like the back of his hand. He makes regular checks of bamboo, taking samples for examination in the Wolong Reserve laboratory.*

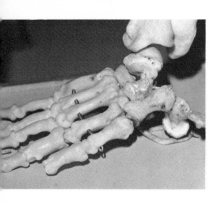

Above, *the skeleton of the hand of a panda showing its unique bone structure.*
Below, *Drawings showing the five fingers and pseudo thumb, known as the 'radial sesamoid'. It is a kind of sixth finger which makes it possible to pluck the tough bamboo cane. No other species has this unique physical feature.*

witnesses. A BBC television programme on pandas in 1984 gave a figure of 800. A leading scientist, known to be a stickler for facts, admitted that in seventeen years of association with 'panda activities' he had yet to see a live one in the wild. When the BBC's John Craven took his 'Newsround' camera team to the Wolong reserve in 1986, his guide told him that he had seen only two pandas in nearly three years. On-the-spot biologists also admit to having seen not more than forty or fifty since the late 1970s. The truth is that no shred of evidence exists to justify an optimistic view. As the *Ta Kung Pao*'s editorial put it: 'Time is running out rapidly for China's most traditional animal. There can be only a few hundred of them left.' That was forty-one years ago!

To remove the threat of the withering bamboo groves, the scientists are now introducing other bamboo species from southern Sichuan to form mixed groves and to cross the plant with other varieties so as to breed a new non-withering kind to replace it as the panda's staple diet.

But all is not gloom. There are some fortunate pandas which never suffer the bamboo crisis. They are not many but the fact remains that they *do* exist.

These can be found around Dafengding on Mount Daliang. Scientists have explained that geographic conditions in the area account for this happy state of affairs. Located on the southern edge of Yunnan-Guizhou highland, Mount Daliang enjoys a warm temperature that supports the growth of several species of bamboo that are to the pandas' taste. They can, therefore, always find something to eat. If one variety flowers the pandas merely switch to other kinds.

In singling out bamboo as the panda's major food, nature took pains to equip the animal with a pseudo thumb, known as the 'radial sesamoid'. In reality it is a kind of sixth finger, and without it pandas could not hope to pluck the tough bamboo cane which contains life-giving nutrient, and hold it comfortably. No other animal possesses this unique phsyical feature which is an invaluable asset to the Giant Panda.

# CHAPTER TEN

# The Peril of Snares

THE GIANT PANDA IS PROTECTED BY LAW, WHICH means two years in prison for anyone caught trapping the animal either for its pelt or as food. The *Daily Telegraph* ran a front-page story quoting the Chinese official *People's Daily* when a Sichuan peasant was given the statutory two years for killing a panda for food. It took less than half-an-hour for the court to find him guilty.

Alas, however, there are many poachers actively engaged in the Sichuan forest setting their countless snares – not for pandas but bigger and more lucrative game. The musk glands of deer fetch high prices in the world of Chinese traditional medicine. This, then, is their target. Sadly, many a panda is known to fall foul of the iron jaws of these concealed traps. Dr George Schaller is the director of Wildlife Conservation International, New York Zoological Society, who tirelessly leads the World Wildlife Fund's team of scientists in their joint campaign with Chinese conservationists to save the panda from extinction. He is known to be deeply concerned about this menace, which he has described as 'the most serious threat facing pandas'. Rightly, he advocates some form of control.

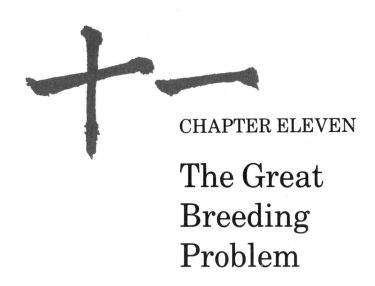

CHAPTER ELEVEN

# The Great Breeding Problem

HEALTHY PROCREATION OF ANY SPECIES IS VITAL TO ITS survival – but pandas have an abnormally slow rate of breeding compared to most other animals in the wild. The reason is a very simple one. Male and female live apart. The panda 'family' does not exist. Hence the ancient Chinese name for pandas – 'hermits of the forest'.

If mating is to stand any chance of success it is vital for the male's rut to coincide with *estrus* (heat) in the female. Estrus involves an increase of oestrogen hormones in the female's bloodstream and it is now that the male's sperm should be at its peak. Nor must it be forgotten that, in any event, the period of receptivity is between one and three days.

It used to be the accepted belief that females came into estrus twice a year, until Dr Devra Kleiman, deputy-director at Washington Zoo carried out a carefully planned experiment. She initiated a 'panda log' with a team of volunteers to monitor day and night activities of the zoo's pandas, 'Ling-Ling' and 'Hsing-Hsing, and record their behaviour. This vigil led to the discovery that estrus came generally only once a year and was confined to a period of time lasting from ten to eighteen days mostly through the months April to June, though starting in March with zoo pandas.

Nevertheless, not everyone was – or is even now –

fully convinced that the females are mono-estrus. Some Chinese experts say that the Spring produces peak estrus twice and also a faint hint returns in the autumn! Dr Desmond Morris pointed out that 'Chi-Chi' at London Zoo also showed symptoms of estrus at this late time of the year.

Sometimes the female will miss the estrus period completely. An example of this is the Japanese female 'Huan-Huan' who, said her keepers, displayed no sign of it for two years running, 1983 and 1984. Then again, the estrus period is normally also bypassed when birth has taken place. Yet, contrary to this rule, Chapter Twenty describes the extraordinary performances by Chengdu Zoo's 'Mei-Mei', prima donna of all panda mums, between 1980 and 1986.

Females reach sexual maturity earlier than males and come into season for the first time at two and a half to three and a half years of age, or about three years sooner than the male.* Estrus increases in intensity to a peak at twelve years of age diminishing around eighteen. This again recalls Tokyo's 'Huan-Huan' who gave birth in June 1986 when she was, unbelievably ... sixteen years old! Truly remarkable. Small wonder that the Japanese were overjoyed.

The low, deep mating calls echo through the forests beginning with moans, bleats, and occasional barks when an interested male is around. These calls are sometimes accompanied by displays of aggression like pawing, swatting, squealing or even snapping. She will also rub her anal scent glands on hard objects. At this stage the male should emit a series of bleats. Without this response it is almost certain that mating will not take place. This behaviour, however, does not necessarily mean that mating is taking place or is about to. The ultra-shy female panda is one of the animal world's most selective creatures. In the love cycle of the panda it is the female who has the prerogative of choice.

*The first mating at Mexico Zoo in 1980 took place when both pandas were five years old.

*Pandas mating at Beijing Zoo.*

*She's huge – but is she pregnant? There's no telling because the foetus is infinitesimally small.*

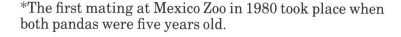

Females are even suspected of abstaining from mating for some years.

After the 'love song' has attracted suitors and the female makes up her mind who will be her 'Romeo', nothing can then change the situation. The mating pandas may even climb a tree to ensure conjugal privacy. Once mating is over the male may disappear for ever. In the autumn when panda births take place, after a gestation which may vary from about ninety-five to 160 days, the female will seek out a hollowed tree or cave which passing predators are unlikely to notice. She will take great pains to line this temporary home with leaves and moss. Failure to find such a haven will induce her to use her powerful teeth to chew away at a broad trunk painstakingly for several hours until such a maternity home is ready for occupation. She will even add the small mountain of sawdust to the soft bedding of leaves and moss! An eye-witness actually watched such a home being made (see pages 65–7). This accounts for the number of hollowed trees to be seen in these forests.

A normal litter may consist of one or two, sometimes even three – but only one will survive. The mother will automatically reject the other(s) because of the intensive maternal care required during the first few months, much of which centres on constant cradling and embracing, which are unique features in the mother-child relationship and will occupy eighteen to twenty hours a day for the first few weeks and then continuing periodically for months. The abandoned one(s) will perish from the night cold if for no other reason. There is no deviation from this rule of nature where pandas are concerned.

Once the female has given birth, she will miss her estrus the following year but, if the cub should die, the female may return to estrus the following spring. It has been said that a mature female is lucky if she succeeds in raising a cub every three years in the wild.*

---

*Beijing and Chengdu Zoos have exceeded this by far (see pages 89–90).

*You can see how small the baby panda is in relation to his mother.*

The new-born is 900–1000 times smaller than its mother, usually about 10 cm long and weighing only 100 gram, which is about equal to a medium-size tomato. One more thing is certain – its early screams will be heard twenty metres away!

From now we discover how abnormally slowly all cubs develop; slower than eighty-five per cent of all other species in the animal kingdom. Until maturity – which in the male is so very slow – the absence of mating is one more vital factor which contributes to an all-round diminishing birth rate.

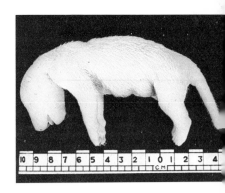

*One who did not make it.*

Taking into account the panda's average life span, – twenty-five years in the wild, only twenty in captivity – this late maturity curtails the panda's breeding life to about ten to twelve years with, of course, limited pregnancies and then only *if* 'madame' is not too choosy; because the female ceases to bear at around the age of sixteen. The balance of new life is, therefore, irrevocably outweighed by the laws of nature which no scientific expertise can affect. There is no magic wand.

Chinese scientist Woo Feng-li has said: 'No other species in the whole world has been dealt such a raw deal by Mother Nature. The panda is trapped by a cruel set of circumstances that lessen all chances of a thriving population increase.'

Chinese and Western scientists have given much thought to the question of artificial insemination, on the face of it an exciting possibility, but in terms of birth currency not so successful as had been hoped, and by no means a booster for the falling birth rate (see pages 89–90).


By the time a pregnant female is ready to give birth she has disappeared from sight. Very few of China's panda specialists have, therefore, ever witnessed a birth in the wild. Guo Haukang, who lives on the Fengtong Reserve, is one of the fortunate few.

It happened on 23 September, 1982 when, in the middle of the green nowhere, he saw a panda crawl into a hole in the trunk of an old withered fir tree at an elevation of about 2,500 metres. With her powerful teeth she had chewed out a forty-centimetre hole

and lined the inside with the resultant sawdust and a large pile of azalea and bamboo leaves.

'Taking the utmost care not to be noticed, I could see her sitting inside as if she were waiting for something,' he said. 'A little while later when I returned she began moaning at regular intervals. I realized she was in labour. If only I could have helped, but I knew she must not know of my presence. The next day her cries stopped. Suddenly I heard another cry, more like screaming, and knew it was a cub. The following morning, peering through the tree hole I could see the white baby lying across its mother's stomach, crying and quivering as it was being licked. On the second day the mother left her cub to search nearby for food. Interestingly, she never once took her eyes off it for a single moment as she plucked the bamboo, never with her back to the tree. This went on for several days. Nothing could have harmed the cub, such was her tension and alertness. On the sixth day I caught a glimpse of the cub; its black patches were appearing distinctly on the shoulders and ears and around its eyes. This was a wonderful experience for me!'

*During those first few weeks it isn't easy for the mother to pick up her baby, he is so small and her paws quite massive.*

*No other creatures display more mother-love than pandas. Ardent, almost passionate at times.*

CHAPTER TWELVE

# Fire! Fire! Fire!

SERIOUS FOREST FIRES IN THE WEST ARE GENERALLY reported, sometimes graphically, by the media, but in China, where newspaper space is usually limited to six or eight pages and therefore at a premium, the editorial columns are naturally dominated by important affairs and not least those concerning the Party. Consequently one very rarely, if ever, hears of fires raging in Chinese forests although, in fact, such disasters do take place even in 'pandaland'.

The cyclical flowering and subsequent withering of bamboo presents a constant hazard of major proportions which is ever poised to threaten the panda's habitat.

Dead bamboo groves present a natural tinderbox under the gruelling Sichuan sun that blazes down relentlessly at temperatures rarely below 42°C, without any break in the weather from June to September.

Game reserves are now provided with ponds, and a chain of look-out posts equipped with chemical fire-fighting equipment are manned twenty-four hours a day. Nevertheless, fires continue to menace the forests which, after all, are vast, impenetrable in parts and humanly impossible to patrol adequately.

CHAPTER THIRTEEN

# The Predators

PROWLING THE SICHUAN FORESTS READY TO STRIKE
are the panda's traditional foes – leopards, foxes,
blue cats, jackals and Asiatic wild red dogs.

Defenceless cubs make easy prey – defenceless
because pandas lack the security of closed-in dens,
and, other than the hollowed tree or cave as a temporary maternity home, have no other lair than a
sleeping place under the stars among bamboo thickets or reeds. While a mother panda leaves her cub to
go foraging, it becomes an easy target. Many are
known to become such victims.

Then there are the ageing pandas, also easy prey
for the agile, voracious marauders. On the other
hand no predator, however powerful, will dare to
stalk the healthy, virile panda adult, because of its
reputation for courage and strength. Defending the
cub is the only time a panda displays aggression,
living up to its ancient Chinese name 'Pi-shu',
meaning ferocious and brave. If need be, the panda
can outclimb or outswim many of its enemies with
surprising speed in spite of its deceptive waddling
gait.

CHAPTER FOURTEEN

# Deadly Disease

*A single autopsy produces a basinful of the deadly worms that strike down pandas, and affect fertility.*

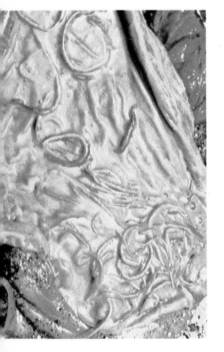

THE PANDA IS HAUNTED AND PLAGUED BY A KILLER which, by a cruel irony, may be attracted by its heavy consumption of bamboo.

The deadly and pernicious round worm, known as *Ascaris Schroederi* attacks up to seventy per cent of all pandas in the wild and, by a strange quirk of nature, as many as ninety per cent of those inhabiting what I would term Père David country!

Once established in the animal's stomach organs the round worms multiply at an alarming rate. Intestines and bile duct become clogged and the intestinal wall perforated. The presence of a thousand of these parasites in a panda is nothing unusual. Professor Hu Jin Chu, China's leading panda specialist, told me how he had found as many as 2,000 in a single autopsy!

'It is always a critically dangerous situation,' he said. 'Animals attacked on such a scale have only a very slender chance of escaping the fatal consequences. Even if the worms don't kill outright, they nearly always adversely affect fertility or the female's estrus which in turn can influence her social and reproductive behaviour. We know that few females escape this nightmare.' Laboratory tests are still proceeding to study the worm's life style and are aimed at solving the problem.

It is significant that autopsies of pandas living in

zoos have revealed an absence of the worm, which makes scientists and vets tend to believe that the pest is attracted by the panda's all-bamboo diet which, of course, is largely absent from their zoological meals.

Wang Zhongyi, associate researcher of mammalogy and head of the zoological section at Peking's Natural History Museum, has this to say on the subject: *'The panda never chews its food carefully. Everything is bolted down. Hence it suffers from poor digestion. Its habit of walking, eating and defecating all at the same time is another thing that attracts the worm. Zoo pandas have a more relaxed existence and suffer no such problem. We also believe that pandas in the wild are known to drink excessive amounts of water and do so to ease the discomfort of the worms living in their intestines. The round worm is certainly a peril which we cannot afford to overlook.'*

*Dr George Schaller and his Chinese colleagues study bamboo growth.*

*Surrounded by an ocean of bamboo goodies!*

At Fuzhou Zoo in Fujian Province, regular examinations – blood and liver function tests, electrocardiograms, X-rays, transfusions – are carried out on 'Tao-Tao' and 'Qing-Qing' without anesthesia. At first, however, there were problems resulting from their life in the wild. They would attack anyone approaching and zoo personnel were bitten several times and equipment damaged. In 1981, nineteen-year-old zoo assistant Chen Yuhua moved her quarters into a room adjoining the pandas' cage. Each day she would feed and play with them, with other workers joining in gradually. This won the pandas' confidence and friendship. The pictures on these pages speak for themselves . . .

## CHAPTER FIFTEEN

# Stress

OVER LONG CENTURIES THE PANDA'S ORIGINAL habitat, occupying about a quarter of China, has fallen victim to man's gnawing encroachment and thus with an ever-soaring population (now increasing daily very rapidly in the hinterland) has been shrinking at an alarming rate, so that today only the bamboo forests of *parts* of Sichuan remain.

The mid-twentieth century industrial expansion throughout China is the latest hazard, which in turn begets the stress, which bedevils pandas. Invisible, but openly acknowledged by the experts, its rate of escalation has so alarmed the Chinese authorities that Sichuan's own provincial government has set aside a substantial budget to meet the cost of resettling families far from forest areas to leave the pandas in relative tranquillity.

Requests by international tour operators trying to persuade Beijing to include Sichuan's panda world in their itineraries for wildlife enthusiasts among their clients have sensibly been turned down. The caring Chinese – fully aware that snap-happy tourists tramping willy-nilly through the green silence would be the surest way of adding further to the stress hazard – have turned a blind eye to such blandishments irrespective of the financial rewards. The Chinese are far more concerned with the future security of the Giant Panda than with earning foreign currency!

With China now in the throes of re-modelling her economy, fostering the 'responsibility' system and all-out free enterprise, one further unexpected type of encroachment is rearing its ugly self to pose a threat to the pandas. Ambitious, land-hungry farmers and peasants – let us not forget they comprise eighty per cent of the Chinese population – are now moving deeper into the valleys and drastically reducing the amount of bamboo. A well-placed Party official at Beijing told me in February 1986: 'We must not allow personal greed to rob China of such an important part of its heritage. You in the West have a saying "as dead as the dodo". We would not wish our future generations to say "as dead as the panda!" This problem has by no means escaped our notice. We will never let it get out of hand. Pandas need their bamboo – and the bamboo needs the good earth.' Industrialization and progress mean prosperity for people – but extinction for pandas.

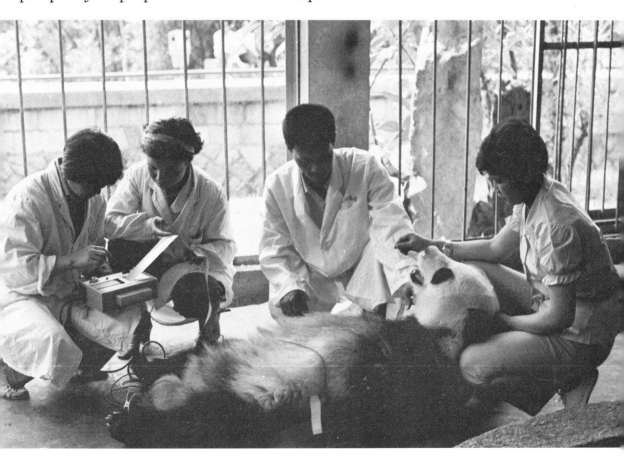

*The bamboo forests carry special notices: TAKE GOOD CARE OF EVERY TREE AND FLOWER!*

## CHAPTER SIXTEEN

# The 'Resting Dragon' Panda Reserve

*Sir Peter Scott leads a team of researchers through a section of Wolong Reserve.*

FAR FROM SITTING BACK, THE CHINESE GOVERNMENT, who have every reason to feel proud of their achievements, have been countering these encroaching threats to the panda's existence for several years with a massive Save-the-Panda operation, sparing neither expense, expertise or effort.

Twelve reserves are established in Sichuan. The largest and most important is the 1,920 sq.-km reserve in the Wolong ('Resting Dragon') mountain area, about a hundred kilometres from Chengdu, chosen because of its reputation for enjoying a high concentration of pandas (believed to be about one hundred), having less human disturbance than other neighbouring areas, which is essential to the shy pandas, and also being well stocked with the vital species of bamboo as well as plenty of watering spots.

Wolong entailed great sacrifices. Nearly £4 million had already been invested during the late 1970s to develop there a promising timber industry allied to furniture-making, both projects providing useful employment. This ambitious programme was jettisoned without hesitation after scientists recommended the area as the ideal sanctuary for pandas.

Its only human population is some 3,000 Qiang farming people of Tibetan background – otherwise about 100 species of mammals and nearly 250 of birds.

By 1981 the Panda Protection and Research Centre had been established in the Reserve comprising six divisions, including ecology, behaviour, biochemistry and reproduction. From here, a combined team of dedicated Chinese and Western scientists seconded from the World Wildlife Fund (which also contributed $1¼ million towards the Chinese budget of nearly $4 million) carries out daily operations – a tough life in the beautiful but terribly remote mountains.

*The breeding farm Wolong with a fully-equipped veterinary station also includes a wild playground of more than 20,000 square metres.*

The nursery now has ten pandas (in 1986), and there is also an animal and plant specimen exhibition room, a deciduous pine garden and a meteorological station. A panda observation and breeding farm has been set up among the lush bamboo groves at an elevation of 2,500 metres. Artificial insemination techniques are studied and a great deal of information has been gathered concerning the conservation of semen and its survival after freezing. To improve results, the breeding farm is adjusting its mating population by sex and age. Detailed records are kept on eating and sleeping habits and the normal round of activities. Special attention is paid to the panda's call during the mating season and to analysis of its sound, all panda cries being recorded. A systematic study is made of disease prevention and treatment. Also playing a vital role in the reserve's programme is a hospital and quarantine quarters.

The scientists study the psychology and behaviour patterns of the pandas by trapping and collaring them with mini radio transmitters with which to monitor their movements – as of spring 1986 eight had been collared – no simple operation when it can entail months of patient tracking in icy or sweltering conditions and painful footslogging at high altitudes.

Trapping a single panda to collar can entail months of tracking, covering a thousand kilometres and more. Difficult to locate, often retreating to alti-

*Fitting a collar radio transmitter to one of the Wolong pandas.*

tudes of 3,000 metres or more, their quarry leads the researchers a merry dance. Once collared, there is no guarantee that the panda will be seen again! It's the price of dedication.

According to Dr Schaller, who by now, as head of the WWF team, must surely have covered several thousand kilometres on foot: 'The radio signals reveal where the animal is, which then enables us to trace its daily and seasonal movements – but it's always a mighty big problem!'

Like the time 'Zhen-Zhen', a mature female panda, was no sooner fitted with her transmitter than the urgent nature of radio signals indicated that she was being wooed by *two* males! The sound of scuffles, blows and squeals of pain were heard by the 'eavesdroppers', as one suitor tried to beat the other off the scene. Then the listeners heard the unmistakable love song of mating. Subsequent observations showed that 'Zhen-Zhen's' appetite had increased and she was searching around for more food – a sure sign of pregnancy. Four months later she gave birth in a hollow tree.

Soon afterwards her radio signals broke off. A team hurried up the mountain to look for her hollowed tree-house. There, and in fine fettle, were mother and cub. The cause of the discontinued signals was immediately apparent. Her transmitter was missing – it had somehow been dislodged. But by the end of the year the cub was missing, never to be seen again. Mysteriously, a subsequent cub also disappeared, presumably sharing the same fate, i.e. from predators. 'Zhen-Zhen' died in 1985, aged about fifteen years.

On another occasion, when Dr Schaller sighted one of his first pandas, it failed to sense his presence – perhaps because of its hunger pangs. Concealing himself, the American scientist watched the medium-sized animal sit down and begin plucking bamboo for a meal. He watched it snapping off the centre stems, deliberately discarding the rest of the plant, and begin to feast with gusto. Schaller took a careful stem-count of the number consumed. After the 194th, the panda took a brief rest, defecated and

*This incredible picture shows a famished cub clinging for dear life to a branch and desperately scraping off bark for its survival. Two hours later it was in safe keeping at Wolong where a vet said: 'A few more hours and it would have been a goner'.*

resumed eating until it had completed a hearty meal of 250* stems. Then it moved on.

Having enjoyed the 'lion's' share of publicity, Wolong Reserve is naturally known all over the world where there are people who take an interest in the fate of the Giant Panda. However, another reserve also exists which has an even greater panda population – believed to be around 120 – and which is also in an historic area. This reserve is at Fengtongzhai, on the other side of Jialin Mountain in Sichuan where Père David not only came across the first panda seen by a Westerner, but also established his Dengshi Gorge Church, which was built on his instructions. Somehow it escaped the wrath of Red Guards who destroyed or vandalized nearly 450 cathedrals and churches during the Cultural Revolution and is now a commune factory.

*The famous WWF logo designed by Sir Peter Scott.*

In August 1986 the Reserve, now with a panda population of twelve, made history with the birth of its first baby, born to 'Li-Li' after a normal mating. Appropriately one of the first privileged Westerners to see the new cub was HRH the Duke of Edinburgh, who happened to be making a tour of the Reserve at the end of October in his role as President of the World Wildlife Fund. When he saw the cub, then nearly three months old still of course, unsexed (a process which can take up to over a year!) one of his Chinese hosts invited him to give it a name. It happened to be such a fine day, the sky itself a shout of blue, that Prince Philip resolved upon 'Lam Tian' which is Chinese for 'Blue Sky'.

Since the 1950s, Fengtongzhai Reserve, which covers an area of 40,000 hectares, has provided most of the pandas for China's zoos and those abroad, now a total of eighty-one, including those sent to London, Washington and Paris. An interesting feature of the reserve is that the pandas live peaceably in the company of golden monkeys, takins, white-lipped deer and 209 species of rare birds.

---

*Dr Schaller described in a *National Geographic* article (March 1986) how 'Wei-Wei', a reserve panda, once consumed 3,381 stems in the course of a day.

# CHAPTER SEVENTEEN

# Famine!

*Blossom of death in the Min Mountains – deceptively beautiful! Any day now the bamboo will die and simultaneously scatter its seed. A barren wilderness remains. It will take years before the plants replenish themselves. Meantime the panda cannot afford to wait, but must find food.*

*Peasants planting out new species of bamboo as part of a massive plan to aid the pandas' plight. These are caring people.*

THE DEVASTATION OF ALL THOSE PANDAS LYING IN A wilderness of dead bamboo in 1976 indicated that this would be a vast barren area for up to fifteen years. The bamboo that has grown since then is only a few metres high, too immature to hold any nourishment. This is not the only ill-fated area, as we know. But the experience of Qin Zisheng, deputy director at Wolong and a specialist in bamboo, in 1982 bore witness to the silent, insidious danger.

In the spring of that year she had climbed the neighbouring mountains to study various species of bamboo. At a level of about 2,600 metres she was arrested by the sight of an ocean of bamboo in the early stages of blossoming. She followed the trail of barely perceptible violet and gold 'death' flowers. The sight continued as far as she could see. It went on for several hours. In her notebook she recorded a few words: *'It is the fatal bamboo menopause.'* After taking samples for laboratory testing she made her way back to base.

Meanwhile, she began to receive reports from longtime residents who recalled having seen the last flowering in 1935! It was a warning of what to expect. Sure enough twelve months later she returned to find the entire area a blaze of violet and gold – in full blossom. Climbing a further 300 metres the same sight greeted her eyes. She knew that death, seeding and the fifteen-year barren span were

78

poised to begin at any time. There would be no more food here until 1998!

Qin was anything but surprised. Only the week before radio signals from the panda transmitters led her team to suspect that pandas were moving around in wide circles which suggested their panic. They were, in fact, searching desperately for healthy unflowering bamboo. Faeces showed that they had resorted to eating weeds and bamboo seed, both capable of causing acute indigestion and malnutrition. The situation called for immediate action.

The disaster continued, and spread relentlessly. Seventeen of the twenty-six principal panda-inhabited counties were seriously affected. In all, some 230,000 hectares of bamboo, (i.e. about eighty-three per cent of the total) died and the afflicted area continued to spread. The situation became so critical that pandas were even approaching the tents occupied by some of the field students, searching frantically for food.

From Beijing came Dong Zhiyong, Vice-Minister of Forestry, to take charge of rescue operations. The State allocated enormous funds to finance the rescue squads, totalling 10,000 men and women, to patrol the forests and scatter the meat of nearly 450 killed and roasted sheep. Huge supplies of sugar cane were taken into the mountains to be discreetly scattered as a lure to bring the pandas down to lower altitudes, so that they could receive proper treatment and food. Feeding posts were amply stocked with

*The tender, loving care of this farm worker restores a cub found starving and helpless high up in the Four Girls Mountain of Wenchuan County, Sichuan.*

*A panda rescue operation team reaches the foot of the mountain after an eight-hour slog. They were only in the nick of time – the victim survived! The teams never hesitate to go out in the worst of weather if a panda is reported to be in trouble.*

*Every panda in the wild
enjoys tree bark, most
especially the Salix.*

*A starved panda cub
found outside Gaocun
Village, Pingwu County,
being rushed to safety by
the county officer in
charge of rescue
operations.*

more sugar cane, apples, cornmeal and milk.

The big problem was to keep people out of the area or the pandas would hesitate to make the descent. The area was sealed off and patrols organized to prevent locals from continuing their habits of collecting medicinal herbs, grazing cattle or cutting timber. Arrangements were made for many to be moved elsewhere temporarily. Finally, observation posts from where searches could be made for starving pandas were established. In general the plan was successful. A good number of animals were saved, though twenty-seven were known to have perished.

By mid-1986, rescue centres had been set up in all twenty-six panda counties with trained rescue teams in every village and forest farm. Central, provincial and government funds now support six feeding centres, twenty-four patrol teams and a medical team of fifteen doctors and vets. Sick or starving pandas are sent to the feeding centres. When recovered, some are released in their habitat, others kept at the centres. Strict patrols stop the illegal cutting of bamboo stalks or shoots, which are popular in Chinese cuisine. Dogs are also prevented from running wild. The duties of these good samaritans are posted on their front doors and they are paid for their work. Concrete signposts in numerous places proclaim PANDA PROTECTION ZONE.

It is now thought that the panda can eat twenty-five other species of bamboo. Consequently the Institute of Forestry is proposing to plant these in different years in an attempt to vary their blooming times and thus enlarge the growth areas. Experiments are being made to extend the blooming cycle, and also to speed up the growth of arrow bamboo, reducing its growth to full maturity down to between five and seven years.

In Pingwu County all schools now have special courses on panda protection. Already this particular county has an incredible record; after seeing a loss of dead arrow bamboo over an area of 130 sq km, the People's Hospital panda rescue team alone saved twenty-two of the animals from certain death.

Few rescuers can surpass the record of the Zhong family of Pingwu County. Zhong Zhaoming, an

assistant engineer of the county's Forestry Bureau, has been studying the plight of lost pandas since 1965. Since then he and his family have saved the lives of thirty-two, of which fourteen were babies weighing an average of thirty kg.

Villagers in remote country areas have undergone an education programme instigated by scientists on the importance of panda protection and how to cope effectively in emergencies. Today they allow stray pandas to stay overnight in their sheepfolds and barns, or watch over a sick animal in a cave to protect it from possible attacks.

Tuan Yilin, a young peasant of Lushan County, Sichuan, heard his hunting dog growling and rushed out in time to prevent it from pouncing on, and possibly mauling, a weakened starving panda that had somehow attacked his lamb. Zhang Haubin, who lives on Mount Maocao, Songpan County, brought a stray panda home to feed it before returning it to its mother. Farmers in Yangjing township, Baoxing County, now hide when they come upon hungry pandas and let them eat from their cropland or vegetable plots outside the village. The stories of panda compassion are legion . . .

In February 1986, Li Xinhu, a peasant woman living in Baoxing, was chopping firewood when she happened to glance up and see a weakened panda actually being swept down the river. Regardless of the icy temperature, she jumped in and dragged the helpless animal to the bank. Others helped to carry it into a courtyard where a fire was lit to warm the shivering panda. As soon as it could move it nipped out of the house and shinned up a tree. The villagers brought meat, porridge and other foods but failed to coax it down. The county rescue team were quickly on the scene. That night the panda slept soundly in the local hospital.

A month later, five primary schoolchildren from near the same district found a panda being attacked by a jackal. Fearlessly they drove it off with stones and then escorted the panda for some three km in the snow until they were sure it was safe.

*Almost a fatal victim of famine, this young panda was found on the mountainside by Zhong Zhaomin, assistant engineer of Pingwu Forestry Bureau. He and his family have saved thirty-two pandas, including fourteen cubs, in recent years. The picture shows his wife, Chen Xihua, spooning a milk and cornmeal porridge mixture into the panda's mouth. Named 'Long-Long' (Dragon Dragon), it was cared for in a laundry basket in their bedroom.*

*A rescue worker is all smiles because three more pandas have been saved!*

CHAPTER EIGHTEEN

# Panda Antics

'*The panda resembles the monkey in personality. It is insatiably curious and behaves like an imp!*'

Tangier Smith

*Carrying a stick of bamboo – like dog with his bone!*

THERE ARE MANY TALES FROM OTHER EYE-WITNESSES to support Tangier Smith's view.

At a wildlife reserve in Sichuan's Nanping County a panda wandered out of the forest and approached local artist Fu Weng-li who was painting a canvas for an exhibition in Wuxi, near Shanghai.

Fu, who had never seen a panda in the wild (this one was about 136 kg, judging by his 2.8-metre height!), was apprehensive. He threw his brushes at the intruder, expecting it to scamper off in fright. The panda ignored the gesture and approached him. Fu fled. Thereupon the panda picked up the canvas and held it at various angles as if studying the picture. After some minutes it gave a loud roar (of disgust?), tossed the canvas down and waddled off.

Then there is the story of Gao Yushent who lives in a cottage at the foot of Four Girls Mountain, famed in China for breathtaking scenery. He came home one day and found a panda munching on some stewed steak. He realized that heavy snow had made it impossible for wild animals to forage and tiptoed away leaving the panda to eat its fill. Two hours later it was asleep on a full stomach. At dawn it was still sleeping. Gao shook it awake and coaxed it back into the forest. The panda returned for the next seventeen days, always finding the dish of food Gao left on a table outside the back door. Finally, he notified the local reserve. Today the panda lives more securely in his new surroundings, sure of two square meals a day.

Three days in a row the Ma family, who live at Ch'un Er, had found their bed slept in and much of their rice porridge eaten, just as it happened in the *Goldilocks* story! Posting a guard at the cottage soon solved the mystery . . .

A metre-high panda suddenly appeared, pushed open the window and clambered through. It made a beeline for a saucepan on the stove and consumed the contents. Disturbed by the watcher, the panda panicked and fled through the window, breaking the glass on its way. He never returned – possibly too shocked!

The north-western part of Fengtong Reserve borders on a lumbering area. In summer pandas regularly join the loggers as they relax in the evenings to watch films! And in winter they visit the loggers' tent in twos and threes to warm themselves and earn tasty titbits. They often take mischievous turns, jumping on to the loggers' beds and ripping up the quilts. They have been known to break the strings of musical instruments and damage kitchen stoves!

*He hears us only too well . . . but, being the shy creature he is, tries to hide!*

CHAPTER NINETEEN

# Panda Mystique

*The Chinese authorities having doubled production of gold coins in each of the last three years minted nearly seven and a quarter million grammes (250,000 oz) of gold in 1986 and introduced 24-carat Panda coins into Britain for the first time. The purpose was to fill the gap left in the bullion market when the EEC banned the imports of Krugerrands. A panda gold coin of one troy ounce was priced at £280 + VAT; of this, £256 was intrinsic value.*

RECALLING HOW THE PANDA WAS BELIEVED TO BE semi-divine for so many centuries, it is perhaps understandable why it continues to exert a powerful mystique that certainly arouses Chinese respect — and strong emotions.

Père David learned from landowner Li that the panda pelt he had seen spreadeagled over his floor was only for decorative and good-luck purposes, but that human feet never walked over it: It was not surprising that the people turned out to greet Tangier Smith and his pandas singing Buddhist hymns and overcome with 'genuine' tears.

In 1980 when 'Tian Tian' and 'Bao Bao' were sent from Beijing Zoo to West Berlin, the Chinese attendants and hundreds of spectators wept copiously. The head keeper was unable to eat or sleep for two weeks. A similar emotional scene was reported by the Spanish Ambassador when 'Chang Chang' and 'Shao Shao' were leaving Beijing for Madrid on Christmas Day, 1978. 'The Chinese were so devastated, utterly heartbroken, and officials at the airport, too.'

Nothing, perhaps, ever equalled the grief witnessed at Tokyo's Ueno Zoo when 'Lan Lan' died on 4 September 1979. No less than an estimated half a million wet-eyed Japanese filed past the empty cage, while hundreds brought floral tributes. Ten months later similar scenes were repeated when the panda's mate 'Kang Kang' also died. A government spokesman said: 'Only the deaths of members of our Imperial Royal Family could have created greater sadness.'

# The Year of the Panda?

AND, FINALLY, HOW DID IT HAPPEN THAT THIS ONCE revered and semi-divine animal failed to be included in the Chinese Lunar Calendar which perpetuates twelve of nature's creatures, one for each year.

According to noted Shanghai-born Chinese astrology expert, Theodora Lau, when Buddha realized he was dying from old age, he requested that 'all the creatures of the forests be invited to come to my bedside and bid me farewell. I would be honoured.'

Twelve came in time before his death – and were duly rewarded by the Chinese Buddhists who named a year after them in the order of their arrival, which was: The Rat, Ox, Tiger, Rabbit, Dragon, Snake, Horse, Sheep, Monkey, Rooster, Dog and Boar.

The story also has it that a panda was nominated to make the pilgrimage. By the time it had penetrated into the foothills of Tibet from the Sichuan forests the lush bamboo groves were thinning out. The panda had no option but to turn back or starve to death in trying to reach Buddha's bedside.

Upon reflection, suppose a Giant Panda had turned up ... Would there have been thirteen months in China's ancient Calendar of Ten Thousand Years?

*The Chinese cannot escape the panda image – wherever they look they find that the panda is there, to sell them products or decorate their homes.*

# PART III
# PANDAS IN ZOOS

*HISTORY IS MADE! It is a Chinese custom that the 100th day of a child's life is marked with celebrations – to symbolise the hope that it will live to be 100! So when 'Ming-Ming', the first panda ever conceived and born in a zoo, reached his 100th day, a party was held at Beijing Zoo. Biologist Miss Pyang Gan, who had looked after 'Ming-Ming's' parents, witnessed the actual mating and pregnancy and nursed the cub, took this historic photograph. It shows the 100-day-old 'Ming-Ming' in the arms of Mr Zheng Shuicheng, colour-page editor of 'China Reconstructs', who later said: 'I vividly recall the cub's sharp claws scratching on my pants and the feeling of his coarse fur. That day I had the honour of being the luckiest man in the whole world!' By early 1987, 'Ming-Ming', now aged twenty-four, was living in honourable retirement at Changsha Zoo.*

CHAPTER TWENTY

# Born in Captivity

BY MID-MARCH 1987 THE WORLD ZOOLOGICAL PANDA population stood at eighty-one. Sixty four of them are in China, which has 150 zoos. Because pandas are so large and bulky and a fully-grown foetus so infinitesimally tiny, it is hardly surprising that births can prove to be totally unexpected.

It was a cloudless day in September 1963 with only a warm breeze peppering Beijing with a gossamer coating of the habitual Gobi dust. The head keeper at the zoo could hear a baby crying in the background as he made his customary rounds. He failed to see it anywhere. His steps drew him towards the panda enclosure where 'Li-Li' and 'Pi-Pi' lived. He knew 'Li-Li' was expecting. She had mated 148 days ago. Could it be possible that she . . .?

'The cries stopped as I went into their quarters,' he recalled. 'Suddenly they began again, but I could see nothing at all. Only after a search did I notice the newborn, looking like a tiny, tiny white mouse in Li-Li's paws. Never having seen such a sight before, I didn't even know if the baby was perfectly normal!'

News of 'Ming-Ming's' birth – the first ever in a zoo – caused a worldwide sensation. Chairman Mao when told is reported to have said, wisely and softly: 'An event like this is one of the good moments in life.'

Since that historic day, fifty babies have been born in the twenty-five Chinese zoos which have pandas. Twenty-seven of them survive today. Of the fifty, twenty-two were bred at Beijing with fifteen still alive. The year 1986 was a record for Chinese zoo panda births, ten in all with seven survivors. The previous best year was 1984 with seven births but only three survivors. Significantly, of today's Chinese population of sixty four pandas, only twenty-five per cent are capable of giving birth! Does any other living species have such a snail-like birthrate today? It is doubtful.

A lack of proven males is one major problem. The males at Beijing, Chengdu, Washington and Mexico are the only reliable ones capable of guaranteeing natural birth, while the new method of conception by means of articifical insemination has seen the best results at Beijing, Chengdu and Shanghai. The first panda to be conceived by AI was 'Yuan Jing' in September 1978 at Beijing where, incidentally, the experts have found that AI usually results in the birth of two cubs, with one destined to die because of the mother's inability to care for more than one at a time. At Chengdu, one in five of all births is by AI. Shanghai's first birth by this means was in 1983. At this zoo it is of interest to note that their four pandas are given regular weekly treats of spareribs which are added to their routine diet. Perhaps it has a beneficial effect, for, as of April 1985, two of the animals were in their nineteenth year and among China's oldest in zoos.

The case history of 'Zheng Zheng', born at Beijing in 1985, has attracted panda breeding experts in zoos all over the world for a special reason. At the age of only eight days and 18.4 cm long, the zoo's panda experts began to rear it by hand, unheard of and never before achieved in pandaworld. Weighing less than 0.25 kg, he was placed in a special incubator for the next three months and fed cow's milk from a bottle. By six months he weighed 14.3 kg and was 89 cm long. Soon he began to drink

*A mother and her cub.*

*Panda birth: ten minutes old . . . and ten centimetres long.*

*The eighth day!*

*At the age of two weeks the familiar black and white markings become prominent.*

milk from a bowl and to chew tender bamboo leaves. 'Zheng Zheng' is now a strapping fellow.

Without any question, the world's busiest panda mum is 'Mei-Mei' (named after the first 'Mei-Mei' who went to Chicago in 1938) from Chengdu Zoo. Born in the wild in September 1971, 'Mei-Mei' has carved herself an indelible niche in panda history by being awarded the unique titular accolade 'Heroic Mother'. From Li Jian, one of her keepers, I have this report of her incredible record of SIX CUBS . . .

| 'Rong-Sheng' | born 1980 | Survived |
| 'Jin-Jin' | born 1981 | Survived |
| 'Chuan-Chuan' | born 1983 | Died |
| 'Qing-Qing' | born 1984 | Survived |
| 'Cheng-Cheng' | born 1985 | Survived |
| 'Junior' | born 1986 | Survived |

The most interesting feature of these births is that 'Rong-Sheng' was born by means of artificial insemination whereas for the remaining five 'Mei-Mei' received AI despite having been known to copulate in the normal way. 'It is, therefore, hard to tell which was the successful method', said Li. 'You see, we weren't taking any chances.' But what a good idea! They were all twin births. In each case only one survived.

Because of the sexing problem 'Junior' will have to wait a while perhaps even more than a year, for his or her proper name. It was twenty months before the Mexican cub 'Liang-Liang' was properly identified, and it took eighteen months to identify his sister 'Tohui', who had at first been thought to be a boy – a sexing error also made in the case of Ruth Harkness's pandas (See Longevity Chart, Chapter Twenty-Two). The Japanese were taking no chances with their new-born cub on 1 June, 1986 so they invited the public to select a neutral name.

Having already pointed out that a female bypasses her annual estrus the year after birth, we should explain that 'Mei Mei's' rare performance was made possible by Director Dr He Guang Xie's policy of having cubs removed from their mother at five to six months and providing them with boiled cow's milk, thus diminishing their dependence on her. This enabled her to build up vital strength.

One might hope that AI would provide an answer to this snail-like growth rate. The problem is that the exact time of ovulation is not known, nor the best time to inseminate, so that, when it is done, it must be carried out two or three times, usually with a day or two between to make absolutely certain. The case history of 'Shao-Shao' and 'Chang-Chang' at the Madrid Zoo, where the first artificial insemination of a Giant Panda was ever carried out in the Western world and also the first time that twins were born in the West, is of particular interest. On 25 March, 1982 the pandas were observed making at least nine mating attempts, lasting 45–90 seconds, accompanied by sounds from both animals and interrupted by relaxing periods of 10–15 minutes each time. But no real mating act was performed. It was decided to inseminate 'Shao-Shao'. Semen was flown from London Zoo. The deed was carried out on 27 March and 159 days later on 4 September 'Chu Lin', a male, and a sister were born, the latter dying from neglect seventy hours later.

There are some experts who firmly believe that transferring males from one zoo to another for mating has the very opposite effect. The visitor, no longer at home in his own territory, loses all dominance and confidence. In support of this theory are the classic failures of London's 'Chia-Chia' with females in the Washington and Moscow zoos.

The method employed at Chapultepec Zoo Park, in Mexico, is significant. When 'Ying-Ying' and 'Pepe', both not quite a year old, arrived in September 1975, they were kept in quarters specially built for them. They had lived together in China which accounted for their total compatability. However, once they were five years old and at the mating stage, Director Jean Schoch made sure they were separated three or four weeks before showing amorous signs. He did this deliberately, on the premise that over-familiarity induced lethargy, indifference and an absence of sexual motivation. It paid off.

*Madrid's 'Chu lin' climbing.*

*Getting measured for a new suit? He's exactly twenty-eight Chinese centimetres from the top of his head to the tip of that ever-so-tiny tail.*

# A Panda's Growing-Up Chart

| | Weight in grams | Length in centimetres | |
|---|---|---|---|
| BIRTH | 142 g | 10 cm | 900 to 1,000 times smaller than mother. |
| 10 DAYS | 396 g | 12.5 cm | Suckles fourteen times daily. The black fur patches faintly visible. Colouring comes in order: eyes, ears, paws, arms, back and hind legs. |
| 1 MONTH | 1.36 kg | 21.9 cm | Suckles six/twelve times. Mother always cradling it. Crawls only to suckle. Responsive to light but eyes are unseeing. |
| 2 MONTHS | 3.18 kg | 42.5 cm | Suckles six/eight times. Back limbs now support the body. Crawling a little but clumsily. |
| 3 MONTHS | 5.45 kg | 50 cm | Suckles four/six times. Back limbs supportive. A few steps possible. Teeth begin to appear. |
| 4 MONTHS | 7.49 kg | 62.5 cm | Suckles three/four times. Beginning to take few firm steps. Now making a few rolls on the ground and enjoying the new sensation. |
| 5 MONTHS | 10.44 kg | 81.3 cm | Suckles two/three times. Moves around a little but still unsteady. Begins eating bamboo under mother's guidance. |
| 6 MONTHS | 12.60 kg | 91.5 cm | Suckles about twice daily. Running around eating bamboo unaided. Has about twenty-five well-formed milk teeth and a tail of nearly 7.5 cm. |

So now a panda is fully weaned. By one year it is also fully independent, with a complete set of teeth. It will reach maturity about the age of six, but less if female.

*The author is grateful to Professor Hu for his assistance in providing these vital statistics.*

CHAPTER
TWENTY-ONE

# Messengers of
Friendship

ALTHOUGH PANDAS ARE MORE PRECIOUS THAN GOLD dust, the Chinese government with characteristic generosity, has presented twenty-four to several countries in recent years. Cited by their donors as 'Messengers of Friendship', only twelve survive today plus five cubs born in their new homes. These pandas are to be found at London (1), Paris (1), West Berlin (1), Washington (2), Pyongyang in North Korea (2), Mexico (2 + 3 cubs), Madrid (1 + 1 cub), and Tokyo (2 + 1 cub). This brings the panda population outside China to seventeen.

The first and only baby birth of 1986 was at Ueno Park Zoo, Tokyo on 1 June, which suggests abnormally early mating. Such is the Japanese passion for pandas that the Nippon Telegraph and Telephone Co. immediately installed a unique Dial-a-Panda service which enabled panda lovers to hear their little darling's cries, squeaks and grunts. About 200,000 people a day began making calls and the telephone company had to quadruple the number of phone lines to 168, but still received about 4,000 daily complaints from people unable to get through.

*Having fun at Washington – 'Ling-Ling' and 'Hsing-Hsing'.*

93

*'Ton Ton' at Ueno Zoo Park, Tokyo.*

The service was earning the company about $11,170 a day, according to the Japanese newspaper *Asahi Shimbun*.

The recording of a woman's voice, in Japanese, answered the phone and explained who the cub's parents were, its size and weight. 'Now let's listen to the first voice of the cub after birth,' and with that the cries began. No sooner had a Washington radio station broadcast the Japanese zoo's number than calls were being received from American pandaniks!

How do the 'overseas' pandas fare in artificial conditions, far from their home environment and climate? From the following information it will be seen that no effort is spared to devise meals to compensate for the absence of the vital bamboo plants that sustain them in their habitat.

## LONDON ZOO

The daily menu for 'Ching Ching' is:

370 g mashed instant potato

300 g minced beef

125 g cornflour

30 charcoal biscuits

Honey, glucose, vitamins, cooking oil.

To this 4.5 kg of bambo shoots added daily. The species, *arundinaria japonica*, is grown at a farm in Cornwall, picked and packed by a troop of local Scouts, and despatched to London Zoo by train. Cost of the bamboo is about £2,500 annually, and the same for its freight.

## WASHINGTON

The diet for 'Ling Ling' and 'Hsing Hsing':

Locally grown *arundinaria japonica*, carrots, apples, rice gruel, dog biscuits, powdered cottage cheese, vitamins and mineral supplements.

## MEXICO

The Zoological Gardens of Chapultec provide for 'Pe-Pe' and 'Ying-Ying':

| | | |
|---|---|---|
| 3.5 litres milk | 450 g beef* | |
| 400 g rice | 100 g spinach | |
| 1 kg apples | 15 g bran | } Served twice daily |
| 200 g carrots | 30 g sugar | |
| 450 g chicken* | 1½ eggs | |

Plus plenty of locally grown bamboo

'Tohai'

| | |
|---|---|
| 2 litres milk | 300 g beef* |
| 250 g rice | 60 g spinach |
| 600 g apples | 10 g sugar |
| 100 g carrots | 1½ eggs |
| 15 g bran | 3 kg bamboo |
| 300 g chicken* | |

'Liang-Liang' and 'Xiu-Hua'

| | |
|---|---|
| 1.5 litres milk | 40 g spinach |
| 200 g rice | 5 g bran |
| 400 g apples | 5 g sugar |
| 80 g carrots | ½ egg |
| 225 g chicken and beef | 2 kg bamboo |

For the first few months on being given bamboo he would play with it! Now it is part of his diet – about 2 kg.

*Mother and cub.*

---

## MADRID

At the Zoo de la Casa de Campo the pandas are fed four times a day with a gruel made up with the following:

---

*The chicken is served in the mornings, beef in the evenings, or vice versa.

*'Shao-Shao' nurses her baby 'Chu-Lin' at Madrid Zoo.*

1.6 litres milk

200 g boiled rice

250 g dietetic compound (proteins, vitamins and minerals)

150 g cereals compound

20 g yeast

5 g salt

1 egg

½ a yoghourt

20 g calcium caseinate

1 teaspoon honey

In addition they have 1 kg apples, 0.5 kg carrots and bamboo (*Sinarundinaria japonica*) grown at the zoo. When supplies are low bamboo is obtained from Galicia in the green north-western part of Spain where it grows easily.

The above diet is for 'Chiang-Chiang' and his off-spring 'Chu Lin', whose mother 'Shao Shao' died in September 1983 (nineteen days after his birth). Chu Lin now lives with his father, being the first time in Western world zoos that two male pandas have been put together.

## JAPAN

The pandas at Tokyo's 105-year-old Ueno Zoo also do very well. A twice-daily gruel contains:

200 g cooked rice

2 eggs

1000 ml milk

20 g prunes

60 g boiled horse meat

400 ml horse meat soup

50 g sugar

2 g salt

20 g bone meal

2.5 g multiple vitamins

4 g vitamin E

2 g apples

200 g carrots

400 g steamed dumpling, which is made of corn meal,

200 g soybean meal,

100 g salt, bone meal and 200 ml of milk.

1000 g sugar cane

500 g rice straw

Other ingredients according to season are persimmon, boiled sweet potato and bamboo shoots.

These quantities are for one panda given twice daily. 'Huan Huan' does not touch the rice straw.

Once a week on the day bamboo is given, carrot, apple, cooked rice and the dumpling are omitted.

## WEST BERLIN

'Li-Li' receives 250 g of cooked lamb which is added to a soup broth, then served for the remaining six days simply as broth. This contains:

Rice, cornmeal, soyameal, lactalbumin, mineral calcium supplement, liquid multiple vitamins, a tomato, half a carrot and grated Savoy cabbage.

The following solids are given twice daily: about 155 g of South of France-grown bamboo, an apple, pear, some sugar cane and a once-weekly egg.

*Monsieur 'Yen-Yen' tries out* 'Un petit morceau de bamboo', *and finds it* 'vraiment formidable', *at his Paris Zoo home.*

## PARIS

Do we detect a hint of French cuisine in the diet enjoyed at the Paris Zoo by 'Yen-Yen'?

steamed rice        steamed soya beans

compôte of grated carrots and apples

French bamboo shoots     some sugar

vitamins and mineral salt   several eggs

*China's 'HEROIC MOTHER', 'Mei-Mei', wonder panda of them all with her fifth baby 'Cheng-Cheng' at Chengdu Zoo, which is her home. In September 1986 she gave birth to a 6th cub.*

## BEIJING

Here at China's showpiece zoo, where admission is roughly 3½p (!), a straightforward diet is served twice daily for each of the occupants:

rice gruel and maize flour    milk and eggs

minced pork and bone powder

apples                vitamins

4.5 kg top quality Sichuan bamboo shoots

## NORTH KOREA

The zoo authorities at Pyongyang confirmed that their pandas were fed on the lines of Beijing Zoo, but declined to give specific details.

CHAPTER TWENTY-
TWO

# Tangier Smith's Survivors

*Princess Margaret meeting the famous 'Ming' at London Zoo in 1939.*

THE TANGIER SMITH TRIO, 'SUNG', 'TANG' AND 'MING', enjoyed life with intermittent spells between Regent's Park and Whipsnade. Solemn 'Sung', who made an incompatible companion for 'Tang', having been wrongly sexed, died after a year following convulsions from what it later transpired was a spinal disease, possibly contracted in China. Within six months, on 23 April, 1940, 'Tang', too, passed away after a short illness which had similar symptoms to 'Sung's'. 'Ming' was the one who really led an interesting life in London. Although quarantined at first, she was taken daily by taxi from Camden Town to Regent's Park. Otto Fockelmann said that the sight of the panda's face peering through the window at passers-by made the trip 'almost like a publicity promotion!' 'Ming' appeared on a BBC television programme, was presented to Queen Mary during a visit to the zoo, and towards the end of May, the dying Tangier Smith received a letter from Sir Victor Sassoon which said: 'You will be delighted to hear that 'Ming' was recently visited by their Royal Highnesses Princess Elizabeth and Princess Margaret who have both obviously fallen in love with him.' When 'Ming' died in 1944 *The Times* reported it in a five-line paragraph on a page which was bulging with vital war news.

But it was 'Happy', now the property of Ruhe and Fockelmann, whose life was the most colourful of all. Shipped to Germany, he spent two months at the Berlin Zoo, where he certainly caught the fancy of the Goebbels children, whose father, Hitler's Minister for Propaganda, encouraged their weekly visits and arranged for the broadcasting media to cover two of them. After appearances at the zoos in Cologne, Leipzig, Munich, Frankfurt and Paris, he spent the last few weeks at the Hanover Zoo, which the company owned, before being shipped from Hamburg to New York (in the company of Egyptian camels and dromedaries). The New York Zoological Society felt that Louis Ruhe's asking price of $10,000 was too much. When St Louis Zoo heard that a 'real live panda' was for sale they held a Board meeting and 'Happy' was theirs for $5,000.

*Tangier Smith's 'Happy' at St Louis Zoo.*

# ST LOUIS' GIANT PANDA

Arrives in the New World and Goes Into a Fit of Sulks –
But Normally It Has a Sunny Temper and Behaves
Like a Friendly Kitten

He made his debut on 26 June, 1939, doubling the normal 20,000 Sunday attendance figure. And, like 'Ming' at Regent's Park, he was responsible for the zoo's switchboard being jammed with calls. St Louis was in the grip of Pandamania!

Weighing 114 kg, 'Happy' was insured at Lloyd's of London for £3,000 and later acquired a fellow panda friend, 'Pei-Pei', aged seven months, which had been donated by a Mr and Mrs William Schultz, of Ferguson, Missouri.

When he died in March 1946 at the age of ten from heart disease, the St Louis Zoo proposed an unusual offer to the Chinese authorities. In exchange for China's annual quota of two pandas, they would provide scholarships at Washington University, four years fully paid, including keep, for two Chinese students. The offer of such a swap was not taken up. The Sichuan Governor ruled that pandas were more precious than free education!

# Longevity Chart of Pandas Outside China

| Name and sex | | Final home | Arrival date | Estimated age (months) | Weight (kg) | Death | Zoo life span (yrs/mths) | Total longevity (yrs/mths) |
|---|---|---|---|---|---|---|---|---|
| 1 Su Lin 'Happy Moment' | F (M)* | Chicago | 8.2.1937 | 4 | 6.35 | 1.4.1938 | 1/2 | 1/6 |
| 2 Mei Mei 'Beautiful' | M (F)* | Chicago | 12.2.1938 | 9 | 22.7 | 3.8.1942 | 4/6 | 5/3 |
| 3 Chang 'Strong' | M | Died on ship | — | — | 50.0 | — | — | |
| 4 Pandora | F | New York | 10.6.1938 | 7 | 35.0 | 13.5.1941 | 2/11 | 3/6 |
| 5 Ming 'Bright' | F | London | 24.12.1938 | 10 | 25.4 | 26.12.1944 | 6/0 | 6/10 |
| 6 Tang | M | London | 24.12.1938 | 18 | 68.1 | 23.4.1940 | 1/4 | 2/10 |
| 7 Sung | M | London | 24.12.1938 | 18 | 68.1 | 18.12.1939 | 1/0 | 2/6 |
| 8 Grandma | F | London | 24.12.1938 | 19 | 72.6 | 9.1.1940 | 0/1 | 1/8 |
| 9 Chang 'Strong' | M | Died on ship | — | — | — | 18.11.1938 | — | — |
| 10 Happy | M | St Louis | 24.6.1939 | 24 | 118.0 | 10.3.1946 | 6/9 | 8/9 |
| 11 Pan | M | New York | 1.5.1939 | 11 | 32.68 | 5.5.1940 | 1/0 | 1/11 |
| 12 Pao Pei 'Precious Jewel' | F | St Louis | 12.9.1939 | 10 | 28.10 | 24.6.1952 | 12/9 | 13/7 |
| 13 Mei Lan 'Orchid plum' | M | Chicago | 16.11.1939 | 10 | 29.5 | 5.9.1953 | 13/10 | 14/8 |
| 14 Pandee | F | New York | 30.12.1941 | 10 | 28.6 | 4.10.1945 | 3/9 | 4/7 |

| No. | Name | Sex | Location | Date | Age (months) | Weight | Date | | |
|---|---|---|---|---|---|---|---|---|---|
| 16 | Lien Ho 'Union' | M | London | 11.5.1946 | 7 | 18.16 | 22.2.1950 | 3/9 | 4/4 |
| 17 | Ping Ping 'No Danger' | M | Moscow | 18.5.1957 | 24 | 94.83 | 29.9.1961 | 4/0 | 6/0+ |
| 18 | Chi Chi 'Strange' | F | London | 26.9.1958 | 16 | 55.38 | 22.9.1972 | 13/10 | 15/4 |
| 19 | An An 'Safe' | M | Moscow | 18.9.1959 | 24 | 104.87 | 18.10.1972 | 13/2 | 15/2 |
| 20 | Wu Wu | M | Pyongyang | 3.6.1965 | 60 | 108.96 | 11.11.1969 | 4/5 | 10/5 |
| 21 | Lo Lo | F | Pyongyang | 3.6.1965 | 60 | 91.20 | 25.10.1970 | 5/4 | 10/4 |
| 22 | Lin Lin 'Forest' | M | Pyongyang | 20.10.1971 | 36 | 85.10 | 12.11.1978 | 7/1 | 10/1 |
| 23 | San Xing | F | Pyongyang | 21.10.1971 | 36 | 72.0 | 24.12.1979 | 9/2 | 12/2 |
| 24 | Ling Ling | F | Washington | 16.4.1972 | 10 | 56.47 | | | |
| 25 | Hsing Hsing 'Star' | M | Washington | 16.4.1972 | 12 | 27.73 | | | |
| 26 | Lan Lan 'Flower' | F | Tokyo | 28.10.1972 | 36 | 88.98 | 4.9.1979 | 5/11 | 8/11 |
| 27 | Kang Kang 'Health' | M | Tokyo | 28.10.1972 | 24 | 60.38 | 30.6.1980 | 6/11 | 9/11 |
| 28 | Yen Yen 'Swallow' | M | Paris | 8.12.1972 | 14 | 40 | | | |
| 29 | Li Li 'Beauty' | M | Paris | 8.12.1972 | 13 | 28.0 | 20.4.1974 | 1/5 | 2/6 |
| 30 | Ching Ching 'Green Youth' | F | London | 14.9.1974 | 24 | 5.12 | | | |

| | Name and sex | | Final home | Arrival date | Estimated age (months) | Weight (kg) | Death | Zoo life span (yrs/mths) | Total longevity (yrs/mths) |
|---|---|---|---|---|---|---|---|---|---|
| 31 | Chia Chia 'Good' | M | London | 14.9.1973 | 23 | 50.2 | | | |
| 32 | Ying Ying 'Welcome' | F | Mexico | 10.9.1975 | 12 | 27.0 | | | |
| 33 | Pe Pe 'Treasure' | M | Mexico | 10.9.1975 | 11 | 22.75 | | | |
| 34 | Chang Chang 'Strong' | M | Madrid | 25.12.1978 | 60 | 91.5 | | | |
| 35 | Shao Shao 'Young' | F | Madrid | 25.12.1979 | 36 | 71.0 | 23.10.1983 | 3/10 | 7/10 |
| 36 | Dan Dan | M | Pyongyang | 20.3.1979 | 24 | 82.34 | | | |
| 37 | Huan Huan 'Ring' | F | Tokyo | 21.1.1980 | 96 | 95.5 | | | |
| 38 | Bao Bao 'Precious' | M | W. Berlin | 5.11.1980 | 24 | 60.0 | | | |
| 39 | Tian Tian 'Heaven' | F | W. Berlin | 5.11.1980 | 24 | 50 | 8.2.1984 | 3/3 | |
| 40 | Fei Fei | M | Tokyo | 9.11.1982 | 15 yrs | 91.0 | | | |
| 41 | Ma Ma 'Horse' | F | Pyongyang | 1.9.1985 | 8 yrs | 90 | | | |

| | Name and sex | | Place | Birth | Gestation (days) | Weight (g) | Death | Life span | Remarks |
|---|---|---|---|---|---|---|---|---|---|
| 42 | Xen-li 'Victory' | F | Mexico | 10.8.1980 | 127 | 100 | 18.8.1980 | 8 days | News of the birth brought swarms of Press men and members of the public which so stressed the mother that finally exhausted, she fell asleep over |

| No. | Name | Sex | Zoo | Date | | | | Notes |
|---|---|---|---|---|---|---|---|---|
| | 'Boy' | | | | | | | ...in the Tarahuma dialect of North Mexico – but eighteen months later 'he' was found to be a 'she'!* |
| 44 | *Chu-Lin* | M | Madrid | 4.9.1982 | 159 | 110 | | After nine mating attempts lasting 45 to 90 seconds, mother 'Shao-Shao' was AI with semen from 'Chia-Chia' (London). |
| 45 | Unnamed | F | Madrid | 4.9.1982 | 159 | 75 | 3 days | Completely ignored by the mother, it was immediately placed in an incubator where it accepted a specially prepared milk (Esbilac at 7%) – but in vain. |
| 46 | *Liang Liang* 'Brightness' | M | Mexico | 22.6.1983 | 97 | 100 | | Born by means of Artificial Insemination. |
| 47 | Unnamed | M | Washington | 21.7.1983 | 125 | — | 3 hours | Although semen from 'Chia Chia' (London) was AI in the event of the parents' copulation proving unsuccessful, it proved to be unnecessary! The cub was expelled from the vagina 'almost like a missile', the birth report said. |
| 48 | Stillborn | M | Washington | 5.8.1984 | 134 | — | Nil | Delivery appeared more normal than above, with contractions every 20 minutes during the 2 hours prior to delivery – but stillborn. |
| 49 | Xia-Hua | F | Mexico | 19.8.1985 | 90 | 78 | | Also born by means of AI, about which this zoo has acquired much expertize. Natural conception. No weight taken. Mother refused to let keepers near to the cub. |
| 50 | Ton-Ton | ? | Tokyo | 1.6.1986 | 121 | — | | Ueno Zoo gave no details of the cub's birthweight. Its weight was published at 5 months (5.25 kg). Ton-Ton was chosen by public ballot as a 'neutral name' because its sex was not known. |

*The sexing muddles. Pandas are difficult to sex accurately. Of those listed in this Longevity Chart, numbers 1, 2, 7, 14, 16, 18 and 28 were incorrectly determined. Perhaps one of the most amusing mix-ups was at London Zoo where 'Lien Ho' and the memorable 'Chi Chi' were identified as female and male respectively. But 'Chi Chi's' male status, which had been confirmed by a noted scientist, proved to be wrong six years later when 'he' was anaesthetized for medical treatment! Similar errors have been made in China, too.

The *Longevity Chart* lists six pandas which are not accounted for in our story. These are:

*No. 2 Mei Mei.* On the strength of her contract with the Brookfield Zoo, Ruth Harkness went back to China with a fresh expedition and acquired this cub as a prospective mate for 'Su Lin' – blissfully ignorant of the time it took for cubs to reach sexual maturity. But what a mix-up occurred: 'Su Lin', originally believed to be female, was found to be a male during the autopsy carried out after her death in 1938, while 'Mei Mei', thought to have been male, turned out to be a female!

*No. 4 Pandora.* Her capture was the result of a concerted field operation by Dean Sage (see page 00), a trustee of the New York Zoological Society, and Messrs Dickinson and Spooner, both lecturers at the West China Union University at Chengdu.

*No. 11 Pan.* Of all zoo pandas this was the only one which never settled down and always remained slightly grouchy and aggressive. It had been donated by Mrs Dean Sage.

*No. 13 Mei Lan.* This was the third and last of the Chicago (Brookfield) pandas, originally captured in Sichuan by Chicago *Daily News* journalist A. T. Steele. 'Mei Lan' achieved fame by living for nearly fourteen years.

*Nos 14 and 15 Pandee* and *Pandah.* Given these odd names through a public contest which the sponsors later regretted, the pandas had been presented by none other than Generalissimo Chiang Kai-shek and his sister-in-law. Of all the panda globe-trotters these were the only ones compelled by circumstances to run the gauntlet of enemy aircraft and U-boats after a memorable forty-six-day journey from China to New York in December 1941. It is possible that Pandee may have broken all weight records, becoming a huge 172 kg, which is well above the normally accepted average of 150 kg for a full-grown animal.

CHAPTER TWENTY-
THREE

# To Be or Not To Be – Bear, Racoon – or What?

EVER SINCE THAT DAY IN 1874 WHEN PROFESSOR MILNE Edwards, a man of towering erudition who never accepted any professional opinion contrary to his own views, made the sledgehammer announcement that Père David had erred in identifying the Giant Panda as a member of *Ursidae*, the bear family, when, he pontificated, the creature could not be anything less than one of the racoon group, noted scientists and zoologists the world over have disputed one or the other. No less than fifty-one different phylogenetic treatises have been published by different experts. Their views fall into three categories:

1. The panda is a bear is a bear is a bear, and a 'specialized' one at that.

2. The panda is a 'specialized' member of *Procyonidae*, which are the North American racoons.

3. The panda is out on a limb by itself and belongs to a completely separate carnivore family known as *Ailuropodidae*.

The word *Ailuropodidae* means 'bear cat', and the

*The Lesser, or Red, Panda with its racoon-like face.*

panda's popular Chinese name, *da xiongmao* simply means 'big bear cat', though for long centuries it was known as *bei xiong*, meaning 'the white bear'. Its relationship to the cat family, however, does not seem to go beyond its undeniably cat-like paws. Its many similarities to the bear, especially in its blood serum, have led some zoologists to believe that it must have branched off early from the *Ursidae*, and is, perhaps, a cousin to such long-extinct ancestors of the modern bear as *Hemicyon* and *Hyaenarctor*. Other scientists remind us that many of its habits and the structure of its teeth more closely resemble certain members of the racoon family. If it does indeed belong among the racoons, it is the only species of *Procyonidae* found outside the Americas. The final theory of those in Group 3 is that the *Ailuropodidae* are not related to any of these, but in fact form a family of their own.

After the deaths of the three pandas at the Brookfield Zoo, Chicago (nos 1, 2 and 13, p.100), the carcasses went to the Field Museum of that city and formed the basis for a monumental anatomical study by curator Dwight Davis who, incidentally, had made pandas his major field of study. His conclusion, published in 1964, was loud and firm ... 'the anatomy of the Giant Panda is clearly ursid with several specialized characteristics' (referring, no doubt, among other things to the Giant Panda's highly enlarged forequarters and reduced hindquarters – which account for its waddling gait – together with its radial sesamoid or extra 'thumb' (see p.60), which enable it to sit on its bottom for hours at a time eating bamboo).

Another leading exponent of these studies, V. Sarich, published a paper in London in 1973, which was titled: 'The Giant Panda is a Bear!' Here in Britain our own brilliant Desmond Morris sides with the *Procyonid* interpretation. I fear the argument may never be resolved. So be it; that is part of the Giant Panda's uniqueness.

CHAPTER TWENTY-FOUR

# Pandas are Intelligent

*After washing out his quarters, 'Wei Wei' goes off to fetch another bucket of fresh water. 'Wei Wei', now aged seven, is the world's most brilliantly playful panda. He can ride a bicycle, zoom down a slide and enjoy a game of 'horse and cart' with his Alsatian friend, 'Lo Lo'.*

CHINESE PANDA EXPERTS ARE AGREED THAT, DESPITE their captive environment far from the sight or smell of the yawning bamboo forests of China, Giant Pandas suffer no loss of intelligence. Wang Wan-ming, a panda trainer at Beijing, has only to call the name of his four charges and they 'immediately drop whatever they may be doing and come padding over,' he says. 'They even stand up on their hind legs and give a cry as if they are answering me.' Wang became so attached to his quartet that after his marriage he and his wife moved into a dormitory at the pandas' own pavilion until their son was born.

Photographs show what one panda 'Wei Wei', trained with love and patience (two Chinese virtues), is capable of doing. Seeing is believing.

二十五

## CHAPTER TWENTY-FIVE

# Save the Pandas!

THE PANDAS' PLIGHT HAS TOUCHED ALL HEARTS. FROM every corner of China children send their pocket money mites to Beijing. Workers, students and soldiers from the north-west clubbed together to send a lump sum with a note which said: 'Our donation is a mere pittance but it shows the whole-hearted support of those of us living in the Gobi on the border region.' Six Nanjing factories using 'Panda' as a brand name for their products (see below) sponsored a donation drive among all manufacturers in the city using the same trademark. Response was immediate. The famous Shanghai Performing Troupe gave 'Panda' performances to raise money, over half a million students in the city have set aside a Panda Donation Day, and leading artists and calligraphers have donated their works.

In other parts of the world, too, people have rallied to the cause. After the last massive bamboo die-off the Japanese Government donated nearly £150,000, while the Japanese wing of the World Wildlife Fund contributed twenty pick-up trucks, and Mrs Nancy Reagan was there with her Pennies for Pandas Fund, totalling five million (see page 00) and Jeeps. Nine children from the Panda Preservation Committee in Los Angeles raised the incredible sum of $90,000 in thirty-eight days. They went to China and there '... actually touched some pandas – even hugged them'. Now they are involved in an 'Adopt a Panda' promotion.

---

And now – calling all readers. If you wish to be associated with this display of concern for the survival of the terribly endangered Giant Pandas, the China Wildlife Conservation Association will, I know, be only too happy to hear from you. Their address is Hepingli, Beijing, China. Be sure to address your letter to Mr Li Gui-ling, the CWCA Secretary-General. Or you can send your contribution direct to the CWCA, A/c No 7141141, Foreign Exchange Office, Domestic Dept, Bank of China, Beijing.

The dodo might have been alive today if people had only known about the critical importance of conservation 250 years ago on the island of Mauritius. It is truly miraculous that the Giant Panda has survived to the present day and there is now no reason why it should follow the dodo to extinction. But the real miracle of the pandas will be their survival into the next century.

We have been warned.

---

# Panda Brand-Named Goods

Thousands of Chinese manufacturers use the panda's familiar features and name on consumer products of every description ... panda tinned goods, panda confectionery, panda papercuts, panda playing cards, panda games, panda Christmas-tree decorations for resident foreigners, special issues of panda postage stamps, panda greeting cards – even chopsticks with pandas printed on the wood! Beijing-based Panda Books brings out some of China's best literature. And the only Chinese-made cigarettes with Western Virginia tobacco, which are reserved exclusively for the top brass of China's ruling hierarchy, are, of course, Panda brand.

*Among the many Chinese products which carry the Giant Panda's image are lacey, papercut bookmarks, Christmas cards and decorations in paper and silk for the foreign market, decorated chopsticks and stamps, which are enormously popular with both the Chinese Post Office and the Chinese people.*

110

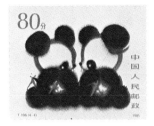

The panda also appears on scrolls and wall paintings and is a favourite subject for toys, both cuddly and clockwork. The Chinese are reminded of this rare and beautiful animal every day of their lives.

# INDEX